L I F E S

The art work, the total art work, involves many aspects of myself, not just one, and they all want to participate in the work. But when the work is done they all disappear, claiming ignorance of the whole affair, and documenting alibis.

–Charles Gaines, *No Title: The Collection of Sol LeWitt*, 1981

Hammer Museum
University of California, Los Angeles

DelMonico Books • D.A.P. New York

LIFES

FAHIM AMIR, HOLLAND ANDREWS, ELKE AUER, KEVIN BEASLEY, NINA BEIER, DWAYNE BROWN, DORA BUDOR, L. FRANK, CHARLES GAINES, LEY GAMBUCCI, PIERO GILARDI, JULES GIMBRONE, PAUL HAMILTON, ASHER HARTMAN, IONE, SHANNON JACKSON, COOPER JACOBY, RINDON JOHNSON, DARRELL JONES, MORAG KEIL, JUSTIN F. KENNEDY, JESSIKA KENNEY, BOB KIL, KITE, WAYNE KOESTENBAUM, RALPH LEMON, ADAM LINDER, OLIVIA MOLE, RODERICK MURRAY, MARIAMA NOGUERA-DEVERS, NIMA NOURIZADEH, OKWUI OKPOKWASILI, PAULINE OLIVEROS, AUBREY PLAZA, SENYAWA, ADANIA SHIBLI, MICAH SILVER, SAMITA SINHA, GREG TATE, MIKE TAYLOR, ROSEMARIE TROCKEL, ANDROS ZINS-BROWNE

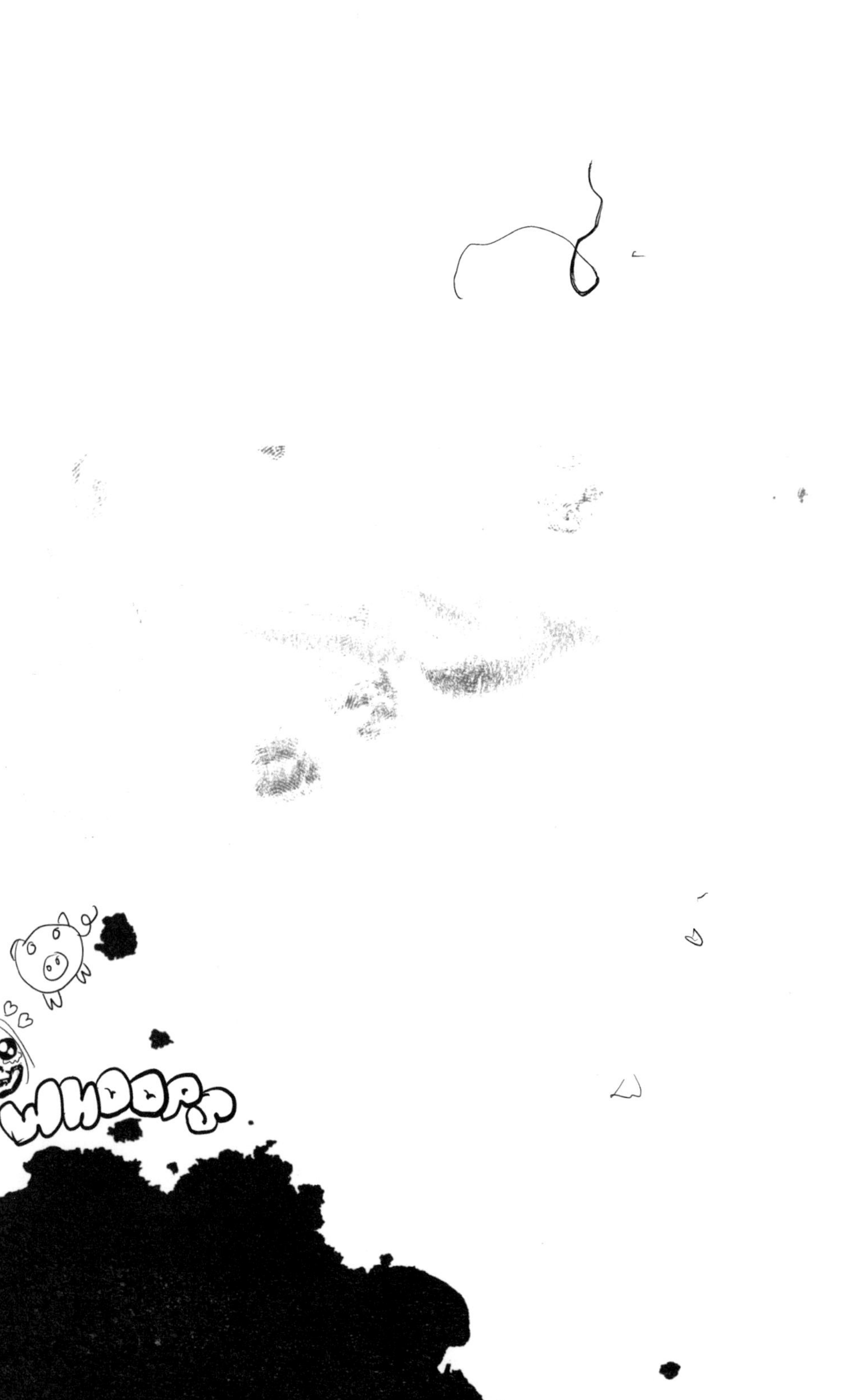
WHOOPS

Director's Foreword

It is never easy to write about an exhibition before it has been installed, before it has moved from idea to lived experience. We can predict and plan, but the writing for a catalogue such as this one necessarily happens well in advance of anything or anyone entering the museum's galleries. Of course, there are preparations that provide some assurances, but things are never certain and are always subject to change along the way. We proceed with each exhibition by trusting the visions of the artists and the curators, and *Lifes* exemplifies this process.

When Aram Moshayedi proposed *Lifes* in a curatorial meeting, I remember saying the exhibition as it was described felt very different from the world in which we were then living. Though the approach he laid out had been on his mind for a number of years, his presentation took place at the height of the lockdown in 2020 caused by the spread of Covid-19. The museum's staff had, by then, been working from home for a handful of months, and the notion of international artists working collaboratively and collectively toward an indeterminate end seemed like a refreshing antidote to the feeling of isolation that had descended upon us. I appreciated Aram's excitement for the project, which he described as being "about the ways in which conversations between artists can produce new artistic forms." Beyond this bold claim, I understood *Lifes* also to be about the relationship between the written word and works of art, how works of art exist in language, for better or worse, as much as they do as objects or experiences. It seemed an inspiring curatorial prompt for an eventual post-pandemic exhibition program. It was a simple enough idea, although it was impossible to anticipate what exactly would be exhibited in the galleries.

I was happy to take the risk. It is the responsibility of museums to traffic in uncertainty and irresolute propositions, just as it is a responsibility to represent, to the best of one's abilities, the sometimes fraught history of art. *Lifes* poses a question Aram has been wrestling with at least since 2018, when he organized *Stories of Almost Everyone*, and I am proud that the Hammer Museum is a place where approaches such as this can result in exhibitions that challenge how we see and think about art. This is particularly important at a time when artists and other cultural workers are deeply questioning the viability and function of museums. At its core, each exhibition at the Hammer reflects a deep-seated desire to change the working conditions of art—how art is made and distributed and for whom and to what ends—rather than accept the standard operating procedures that very often define cultural spaces such as the one we inhabit.

The museum's staff, in particular, has shown how committed they are to the vital work of this institution—namely, the support and facilitation of creative work. I could not be prouder to work alongside such a dedicated group of people who truly believe in the contributions made by artists to our daily lives. This is particularly evident given the changes the world has undergone in the months leading up to the presentation of this exhibition. I would like to thank my deputy directors, Cynthia Burlingham, deputy director of curatorial affairs; Michael Harrison, deputy director of finance; and Fred Yeries, deputy director of external affairs, who offer unwavering counsel and support as the museum witnesses dramatic cultural shifts. My deep gratitude goes to the Hammer's board of directors, which remains steadfast in its commitment to the stability of this museum. In particular, Marcy Carsey, who has served as board chair since 2014, has been an invaluable asset at every step along the way. Our board of advisors plays an important role in the formation of the Hammer Contemporary Collection, and its support spreads among the broader philanthropic community in Los Angeles and beyond, enabling the Hammer to grow and evolve as a center for art and ideas.

We are deeply grateful to Chara Schreyer and Gordon Freund, Christine Meleo Bernstein and Armyan Bernstein, the Danielson Foundation, Karyn Kohl and Silas Dilworth, Leslie and Bill McMorrow, Susan Bay Nimoy and Leonard Nimoy, Mark Sandelson and Nirvana Bravo, Jiwon and Steven Song, Darren

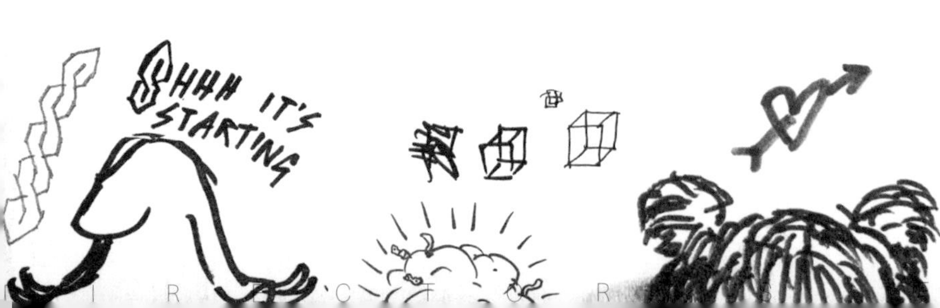

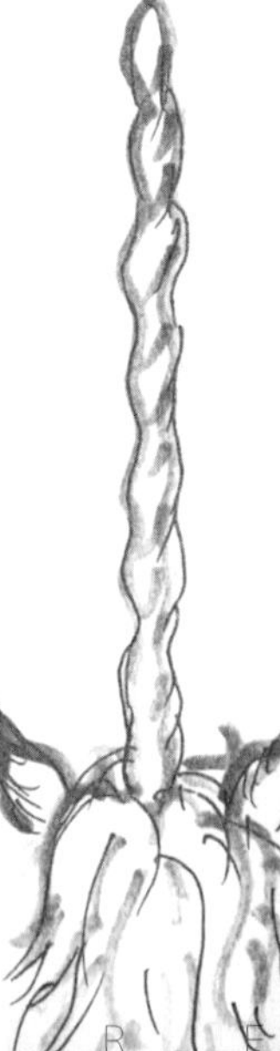

Star, the Danish Arts Foundation, the Knox Foundation, Maurice Marciano Family Foundation, Marla and Jeffrey Michaels, Ben Weyerhaeuser, Ann Soh Woods, and an anonymous donor for making this exhibition and publication possible.

Lastly, *Lifes* would be nothing if it were not for the incredible contributors to the exhibition and publication, whose artistic, literary, musical, philosophical, poetic, and theatrical work is the backbone of this institution: Fahim Amir, Holland Andrews, Elke Auer, Kevin Beasley, Nina Beier, Dwayne Brown, Dora Budor, L. Frank, Charles Gaines, Ley Gambucci, Piero Gilardi, Jules Gimbrone, Paul Hamilton, Asher Hartman, IONE, Shannon Jackson, Cooper Jacoby, Rindon Johnson, Darrell Jones, Morag Keil, Justin F. Kennedy, Jessika Kenney, Bob Kil, Kite, Wayne Koestenbaum, Ralph Lemon, Adam Linder, Olivia Mole, Roderick Murray, Mariama Noguera-Devers, Nima Nourizadeh, Okwui Okpokwasili, Pauline Oliveros, Aubrey Plaza, Senyawa (Rully Shabara and Wukir Suryadi), Adania Shibli, Micah Silver, Samita Sinha, Greg Tate, Mike Taylor, Rosemarie Trockel, and Andros Zins-Browne. Each of their individual practices contributes to a mighty assembly of voices and perspectives. *Lifes* represents a convening of their collective energies, and I offer these words with great anticipation for what eventually will be produced for our viewers and this particular moment in time.

–Ann Philbin, Director

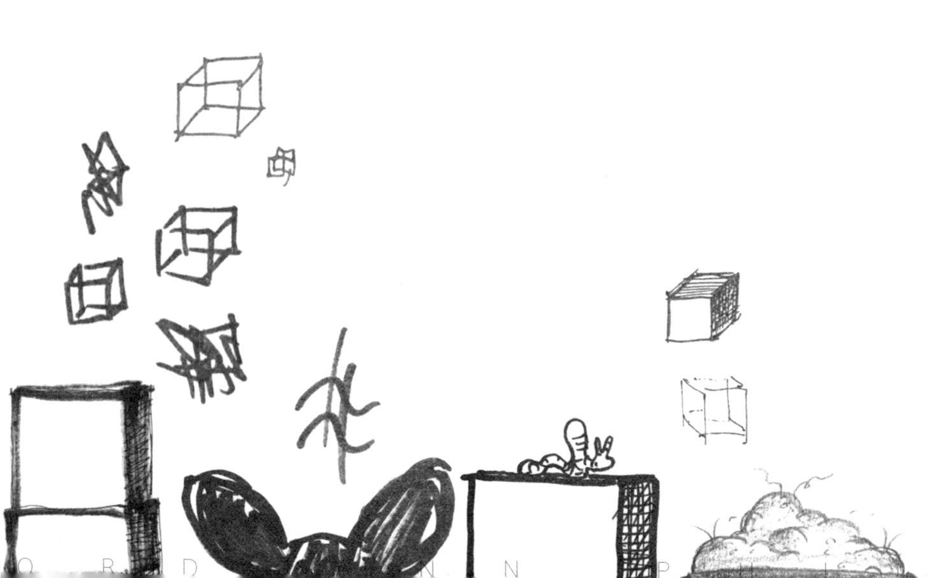

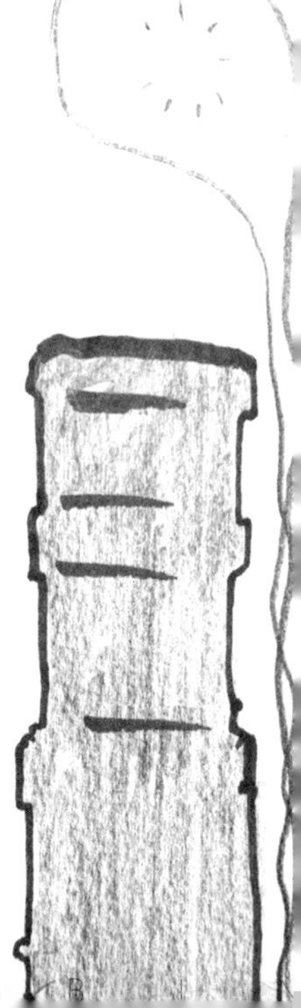

A Text That Dances

ARAM MOSHAYEDI

The contours of this essay begin to take shape in the hands, mouth, eyes, and mind of an imagined reader. Words, when received from the page, have a softness to them. They are quietly rendered; the exchange is intimate. Reading to one's self in an inaudible whisper, the voice may be either one's own or that of an interloper whose vocal timbre is indistinct yet specific enough to approximate someone vaguely familiar. Finding the right tone of a printed text, especially without context, can be difficult.

Words, in the form of sounds, pass through the body; they are stored, carried, and eventually distributed as speech, song, oration, or other forms of vocalization. The American operatic soprano Jessye Norman recounted how the "color" of one's voice is determined.

> This has to do with our own physiological makeup—the shape of the nasal cavity, the lung capacity, the singer's strength and stamina, the height of the inside of one's mouth, the natural position of the roof of the mouth, the height of the uvula, the width of the nose, the distance between the end of the chin and the beginning of the nose, the distance between the end of the chin and the beginning of the collarbone, and the height of the cheekbones and their position near the eyes. All of these things with which you are born determine the timbre of your voice.[1]

Norman awoke to this corporeality as a music student at Howard University, while studying under the direction of professor Carolyn V. Grant. Though she found her voice as a child in the Baptist Church and sang her first operatic aria in junior high school in Augusta, Georgia, where she was born and raised, Norman's embodied identity took hold some years later. The anatomical map she describes charts the movement

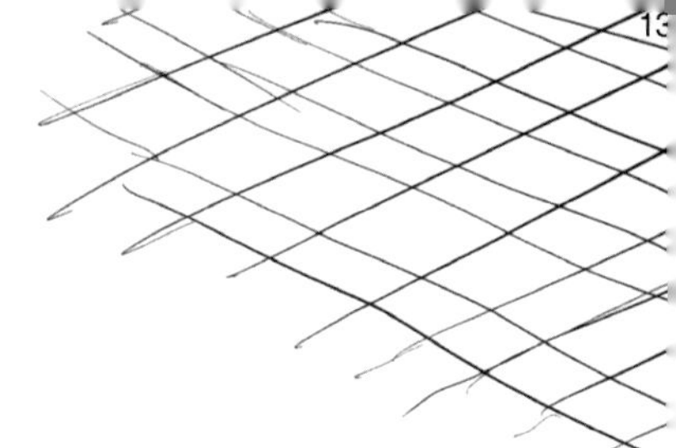

of sound through the body. The translation of words into voice relies upon an assembly of distinct yet interrelated physical properties. Whether read aloud or quietly to one's self, language is manifested in the body—the carrier through which words pass like cargo before finding an external shape.

Writing nearly one hundred years earlier, the celebrated dancer and choreographer of the Ballets Russes, Vaslav Nijinsky, laid out a relationship between the body and words. Written over a six-week period, from January 19 to March 4, 1919, Nijinsky's diaries illuminate the precarious textual and psychological dismemberment of the dancer. Nijinsky was living at the time in St. Moritz with his wife and child and was, by then, an outcast from Serge Diaghilev's company, which had made him famous. In his diaries, Nijinsky was born anew as a writer, and incongruous words seemed to flow through him indiscriminately. Some passages are, expectedly, dedicated to the dancer's falling out with the impresario Diaghilev. ("Diaghilev buys black hair creams and rubs them in. I noticed this cream on Diaghilev's pillows, which have black pillowcases. I do not like dirty pillowcases and therefore felt disgusted when I saw them. Diaghilev has two false front teeth."[2]) Other topics include the benefits of vegetarianism, the quality of his fountain pen, the outbreak of war across the European continent, and the shortcomings of publicity. In his countless non-associative rants, the dancer bounces from topic to topic with such ferocity that it is often difficult to follow.

Nijinsky recalls, "I do not want to dance the way I used to, because all those dances are death. Death is not only when the body dies. The body dies, but the spirit lives."[3] Although he was not even thirty, Nijinsky was clearly coming to terms with an aging body when he choreographed three ballets produced for the Ballets Russes, from 1912 to 1913. His choreography mirrored his apparent death drive, and his final contribution, *The Rite of Spring*, in 1913, remains one of the most physically demanding dances in modern ballet history. The sawing rhythms and violent convulsions provoked by Igor Stravinsky's now-famed musical composition were transposed onto the bodies of Nijinsky's dancers, including Marie Rambert, who danced in the original production and later reflected that Nijinsky was "bent on reproducing every note of the music."[4] The impossibility of this effort and a falling out with Diaghilev in 1917, after Nijinsky married Romola de Pulszky, led to the work featuring new choreography, by Léonide Massine, when it was restaged three years later. Nijinsky's marriage to de Pulszky was a betrayal of his romantic life with Diaghilev, and the younger Massine was to replace him as the Ballets Russes' principle choreographer and as Diaghilev's lover. Nijinsky's subsequent mental anguish was no doubt a result of the loss of both positions—his aged body usurped by an attractive, albeit bow-legged and shorter, eighteen-year-old dancer whose proportions fit comfortably into Diaghilev's bed—blackened pillow and all.

The mythology of the Ballets Russes initially loomed large in the development of the premise for *Lifes*. As one of many apotheoses in the history of interdisciplinary artmaking—a convergence of music and visual and performing arts—the anachronism of modern ballet seemed a suitable foil for understanding the disciplinary conditions in which institutions of contemporary art find themselves today. In an effort to capture any and all audiences, the art museum absorbs any and all cultural and creative forms, for better or worse, into its scope of activities. Dance, like theater, music, and other performing arts, is routinely offered in these cultural spaces, often as an accessory to exhibition programs. *Lifes* acknowledges this, while also bearing in mind that without the museum—as an institution of exhibition and display—none of this would be possible.

The art-historical category of interdisciplinarity is often regarded as an outgrowth of early modernist ballet and opera, within which distinct artistic disciplines and creative practices are delimited according to a spatial and theatrical function in the service of the so-called *Gesamtkunstwerk* (total work of art). This proposed total unity of artforms—a synthesis of poetic, visual, musical, and dramatic arts—was first articulated as a conceptual apparatus of the highest emotive and sensorial

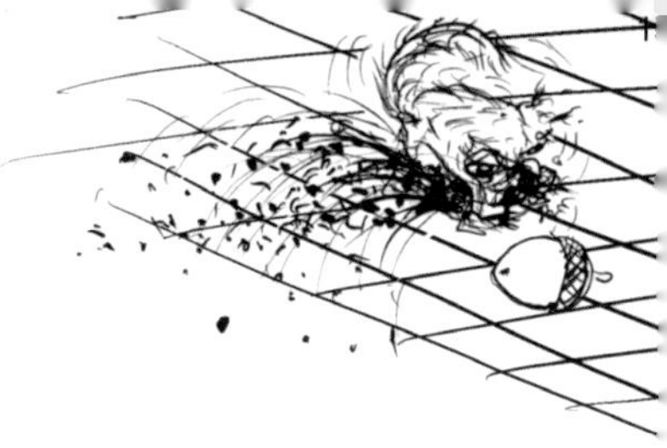

order in 1849 by the German composer Richard Wagner, and it has resurfaced throughout the years since. Though associations with Wagner are often avoided in light of his vehement anti-Semitism and posthumous recuperation in the twentieth century by Adolf Hitler, his vision of the utopian possibilities afforded by artistic unity endures in almost all corners of cultural life.[5] While the Wagnerian manipulation of an engaged, communal audience—those collectively gripped by a feeling of "intoxication"—contributed to the aesthetic program of the Third Reich, it also is a helpful framework for understanding the implications of the global experience economies of the current century.

In 1991, art and film critic Annette Michelson began her essay on the work of Andy Warhol: "A specter haunts the theory and practice of the arts throughout our century: the specter of the *Gesamtkunstwerk*, a notion born of late romanticism, nurtured and matured within the modernist moment, and never wholly exorcised in the era of postmodernism and electronic reproduction."[6] The ghost still taunts the creative industries, willing as they are to embrace such turns of phrase as *transdisciplinarity* and *synergistic collaboration*.[7] In today's well-beyond-post-revolutionary moment, visual artists, choreographers, composers, and poets unite under the auspices of marketing and publicity. Institutions advertise a collaborative ethos, while luxury brands instrumentalize the cult of artistic personality. Has anyone dared to ask: How many artists does it take to sell a handbag?

For its part, the contemporary art museum has in recent years crafted itself as a site of disciplinary convergence, bending to accommodate the varied artistic sensibilities of contemporary cultural life. Programmatically, institutions today exercise a disciplinary promiscuity, blending public programs, discursive activities, and performances into the exhibitions they present. Once considered quiet mausoleums for the internment of supposedly dead artifacts, museums are now teeming with perspiring bodies, sometimes writhing on the floor, making declarative statements, or performing balletic feats in the service of a more activated and embodied form of art viewing. It is by now common to find painting, sculpture, and performing bodies cohabitating in a gallery setting, despite their competing interests.

Of the lasting contributions of the late curator Okwui Enwezor, the impulse toward an exhibition's durational quality was most palpable in *All the World's Futures*—the artistic director's concept for the 56th International Art Exhibition of the Venice Biennale in 2015. Within the framework of what Enwezor called the ARENA, the exhibition facilitated a continuous live program across disciplines, described in the catalogue as "a gathering place of the spoken word, the art of the song, scores, scripts, recitals, film projections, and as a forum for public discussions."[8] The ARENA acted as something of a public plaza within the exhibition. It is where Enwezor's notion of the *state of things* convened most vividly. Isaac Julien's contribution of a dramatic reading of Karl Marx's *Das Kapital* over the exhibition's seven-month duration underscored the critical stakes of Enwezor's endeavor. It argued for a reevaluation of Marx's seminal analysis of economic and social theory within a new era of seemingly dematerialized global financial capital. Situated in the context of a theatrical setting designed by the Ghanian-British architect David Adjaye, the display also staged the conditions of artistic labor in an ongoing moment of political crises.

Enwezor's ARENA is a touchstone for *Lifes*, and it serves as a useful guide for imagining how "epic duration" might function as a weapon against the staid conventions of display. When it was originally proposed, the exhibition now called *Lifes* donned a less grammatically contemptuous title: *Salade Russe*, which suggested an irreverent homage to the Ballets Russes and Diaghilev's penchant for eclecticism and incongruity.[9] Though the exhibition aims to facilitate a cacophony of disparate parts, *Lifes* is more akin to the broken body and emotional void of Nijinsky than the organizational prowess of Diaghilev. It is more a pursuit of new working methodologies than a historical assessment of the *Gesamtkunstwerk* as an

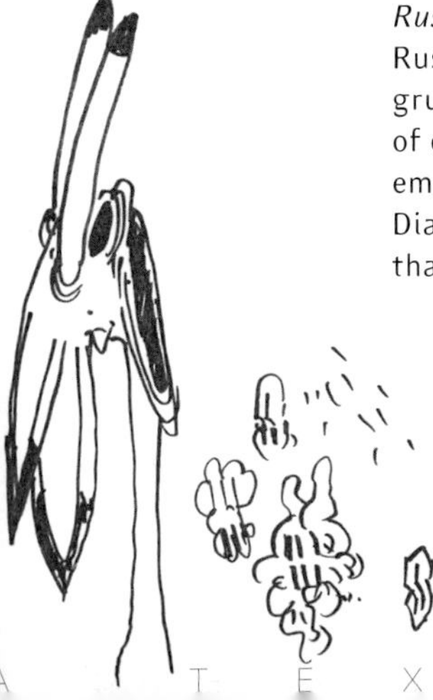

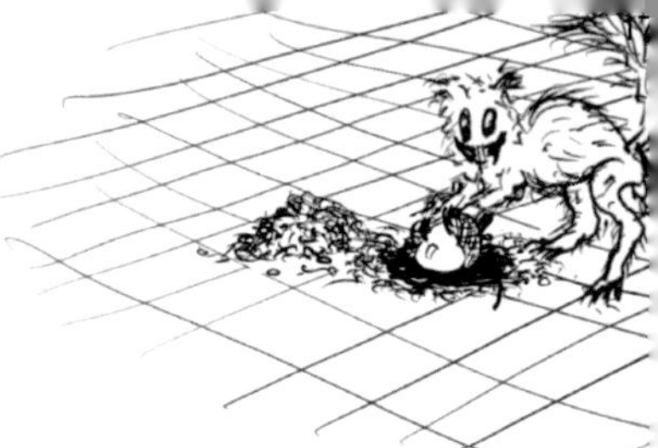

aesthetic category. The world already expresses an abundance of interdisciplinary collaboration; there seems little reason to put that on display further.

In thinking about Nijinsky's and Norman's relationships to language and verse as performers, it became clear that the project should begin with writing. It is no secret that the written word occupies the status of a second-class citizen in presentations of visual art. In a line from *Aisthesis: Scenes from the Aesthetic Regime of Art*, Jacques Rancière describes the intentions of his study, an examination of the "sensible fabric of experience" within which works of art are produced. The philosopher characterizes a blurring of "specificities that define the arts and the boundaries that separate them from the prosaic world."[10] The prose of the world is, for Rancière, something like an inaccessible written or spoken composition that art and artists strive to mediate through the creative processes at their disposal. The allusion to writing seemed appealing as I mulled over how to proceed with an exhibition that would occupy itself in part with the legacy of the so-called total work of art and the possibilities and pitfalls of interdisciplinary art-making. Rancière's discussion of a lecture delivered by Ralph Waldo Emerson in December 1841 and January 1842 drove the point home: "This task of naming is not a work of art. It is not a matter of happy invention. It is the work of life."[11] The exhibition environment is one in which naming takes place, and it is a microcosm that only ever approximates and evokes the chaos of lived experience and phenomena of the world.

It seemed fitting to start with writing—to invert the relationship between text and context—because of its frequent mimetic subservience as a form of response to art. I solicited textual contributions from four writers from different disciplinary positions: ecologist and philosopher Fahim Amir, playwright and intuitive Asher Hartman, poet and visual artist Rindon Johnson, and author and essayist Adania Shibli. The invitations came with no expectation as to how their writing would manifest itself within the galleries of the museum, aside from allusions to examples where language prefigures art—such as libretto, script, and scenario. It was a relatively open-ended solicitation meant to harness their divergent interests, because the desired goal was disparity rather than shared sensibilities.

Our discussions in the months immediately following their respective invitations were centered on the precarious authority words have over meaning, the shortcomings of interdisciplinarity, and the question of audience as a material inseparable from the public life of exhibitions. The introduction of a hypothetical body (namely, the viewer and visitor) to a museum space represents the potential for contamination. This impulse toward occupancy—a public function of the outward-facing, inclusive museum ethos—is necessarily at odds with the museum's mission to preserve and care for objects. The presence of physical bodies in an exhibition space only makes the perilousness of fragile floor- and wall-bound artworks all the more apparent. Daisy Hildyard's notion of the second body—an inseparability of one's supposedly singular body from other physical, ecological, and atmospheric bodies—is particularly useful in understanding this relation. Hildyard writes, "There is a sense of horror which apparently comes from the fact that your body is a physical thing with porous boundaries. Nobody in the world can be completely insulated from the atmosphere; the atmosphere can be influenced by any living body. Therefore each body is involved with every other living thing on earth."[12] The interior of a museum's galleries, then, is just one of an infinite number of ecosystems that must contend with the introduction of foreign agents, specifically a museum-going public whose very presence is counter to the protocols of preservation. Ask any museum registrar about their greatest fear, and, with the sense of horror Hildyard describes, they will tell you hell is other people.

As the process continued, individual writers began to suggest possible collaborators, or intermediaries, through which a conversation around the function of their respective contributions could unfold. Midway through the process of completing "Implied in the ship is the float (My horse is American)," Johnson proposed that we meet with Kite, an artist he'd come

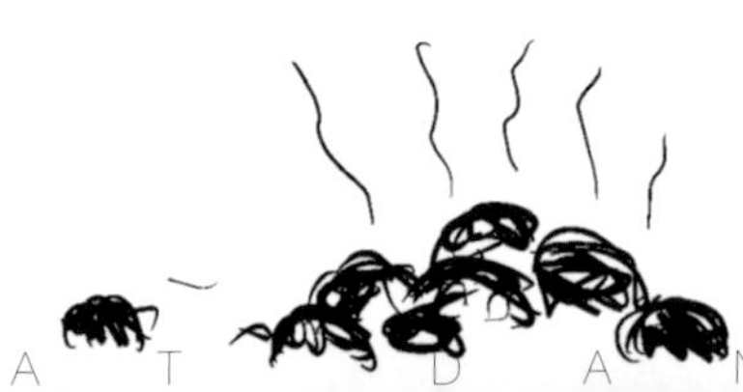

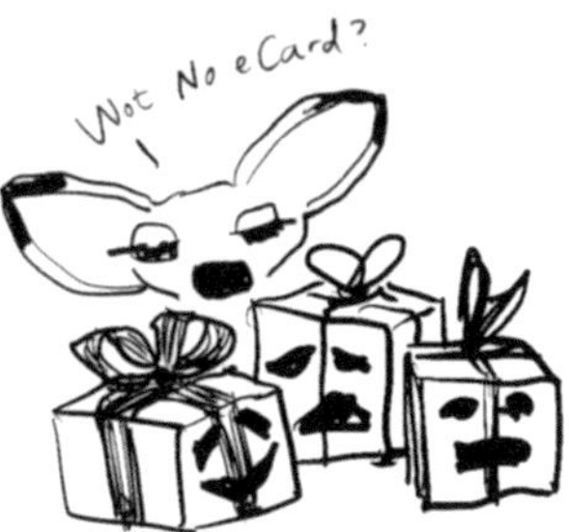

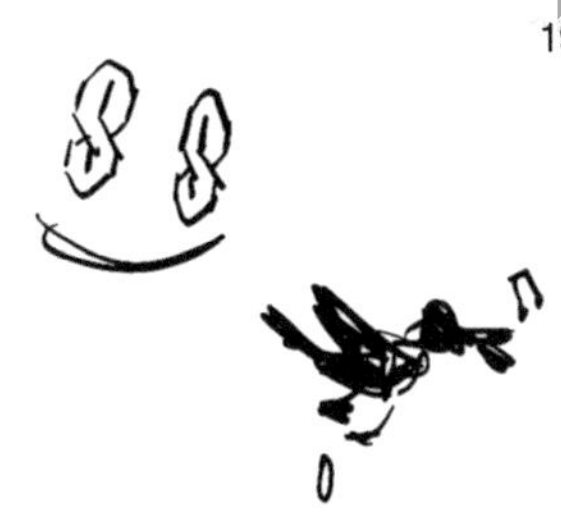

to know when they were students at Bard College. Kite and Johnson's shared interest in Pimu (also known as Santa Catalina Island) off the coast of Los Angeles led us to L. Frank, a Tongva-Ajachmem artist, writer, tribal scholar, and Indigenous language activist. L. Frank's willingness to collaborate bred a more thorough engagement with the geological and cultural histories suppressed by the image of Pimu as an outpost for commercial film production, baseball training camps, and tourism. The creative work between Johnson, Kite, and L. Frank has since centered on an exchange of gifts. Prompted by Johnson's poetic verse, the exchanges between the three artists have helped us consider how and what to exhibit in the galleries. From a curatorial perspective, it has been important to allow the sharing of gifts to be markers of an intimate exchange without necessarily turning them into objects of display. It therefore remains to be determined whether or how the gift-giving activities between them can be adequately represented in the exhibition.

Upon Amir's completion of "Stealing Colors," he recommended a conversation with artist and dramaturg Elke Auer, with whom he has worked in the past. Amir and Auer proposed a tower—modeled on Vladimir Tatlin's *Monument to the Third International* (1920)—that would be a monument for the future liberation of animals and humans. At the time of writing, the specifics of this tower—like much else in the exhibition—are still in formation. This condition of unknowing is what gives *Lifes* its unique character. The organic assembly of discrete parts comes into greater focus as the exhibition's opening date nears, and we also imagine futures well beyond its closing.

Amir also suggested a meeting with choreographer Andros Zins-Browne, whose work I had come to know over the years through mutual acquaintances. Zins-Browne and I began to discuss some of the underlying principles within the exhibition on a broader scale. I mentioned my interest, through *Lifes* catalogue contributor Greg Tate, in considering how the exhibition's organizational thrust might lean on Butch Morris's theory of Conduction, a process for ensemble music-making that merges the structure of musical notation with the

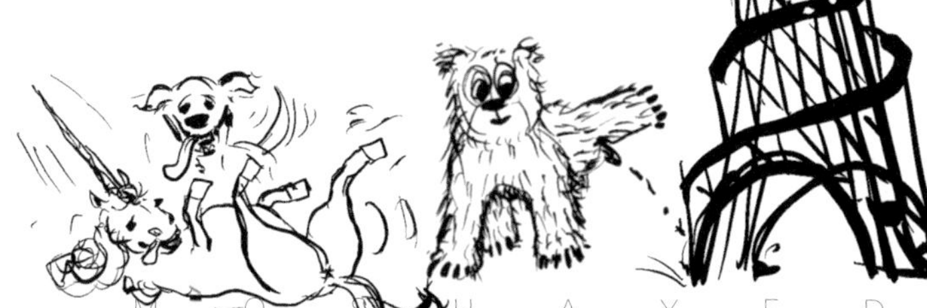

openness of improvisation. As a working methodology, Morris outlines Conduction as "the art of 'environing': the process of organizing people, things, conditions, or influences that interact within, or in proximity to, the work."[13] The conditional sensitivities outlined by Morris's approach offer a refreshing alternative to the historically fraught resuscitation of modernist aesthetics. Conversations about Morris and other musical and movement-based practices that reinterpret the concept of an ensemble have defined my exchanges with Zins-Browne. We have since enlisted Holland Andrews and Jessika Kenney, whose collaborative efforts involve imagining how they might be able to evoke a voice stolen from an as-yet-unidentified performer, who will be tasked with mediating a version of Amir's text in a dramatic, vibrational fashion. True to Morris, multiple trains of thought are unfolding simultaneously in an orchestrated grid of composition, and it will be the challenge of the exhibition to mitigate these respective concerns in the service of cohabitation.

The results of these efforts may produce what anthropologist Anna Lowenhaupt Tsing characterizes as a "polyphonic assemblage," but I am equally prepared for the possibility of dissonance.[14] In a radical reworking of evolutionary theory, Tsing's study of matsutake mushrooms and the political economies that surround them is a useful guide in this endeavor. Although no mushrooms or illustrational distillation of Tsing's ideas will be represented in *Lifes*, her careful consideration of how species interrelate, particularly her notion of contaminated collaboration, permeates all aspects of its planning. Though Tsing and the writings of evolutionary biologist Lynn Margulis on holobionts and symbionts inform the organization of *Lifes*, this is not an exhibition *about* ecology, evolutionary symbiosis, or other metabolic relations. I make no expert claims as to how their theories might be applied to the conditions of contemporary art.

* Except here. Here are some mushrooms. → Growing on dead shit like a boss

Lifes is indebted to the thinking of many other figures. To evoke their influence on the project, I borrow from Rindon Johnson the phrase "discursive helpers." Wayne Koestenbaum's

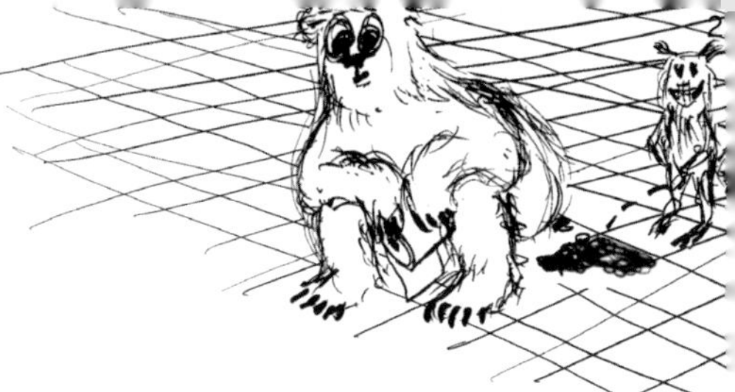

writing on opera is a touchstone for *Lifes.* ("Voice is a room: it opens, for an instant, in a great operatic career."[15]) The Bolivian scholar and activist Silvia Rivera Cusicanqui is another: "The elites adopt a strategy of crossdressing and articulate new forms of cooptation and neutralization. In this way, they reproduce a 'conditional inclusion,' a mitigated and second-class citizenship that molds subaltern imaginaries and identities into the role of ornaments through which the anonymous masses play out the theatricality of their own identity."[16] Cusicanqui is not in the exhibition per se, but her writing on the discourses of decolonization and the subjugation of Indigenous peoples in Bolivia in the wake of multiculturalism and her articulation of Indigenous modernity as an antidote to the linear notion of time loom large. Another discursive helper appears in the writing of Mattilda Bernstein Sycamore: "It's hard to imagine anything more damaging to literature than questions about audience. Then again, it's hard to imagine anything more damaging to literature than literature."[17] Her critical self-awareness mirrors the approach adopted by *Lifes.*

The deployment of discursive helpers in this manner represents an attempt to sort through and collate our encounters with words and with the otherwise private activities of reading. Exposing these influences in this context is a pronouncement of sorts, and it is taxonomical in its motivations. In response to words by art historian Darby English, Fred Moten writes: "Things go together in support of one another so thoroughly that the memory of the thing fades to black, nothing, in dry, exhausted wind. This is the strong theoretical deconstruction of the very idea of one and the very idea of an/other."[18] The inseparability of one from the other, a fusion of critical contexts, and the grouping of seemingly disparate entities and ideological enterprises are at the heart of this exploration. It is as much about how they might come together as it is about the radical potential of incongruity. The museum is inherently a space of anachronism that offers itself as the contemporary in drag.

When I think about choreographer Bob Kil's and artist Nina Beier's animating of Asher Hartman's textual contribution to the exhibition, the foreignness of one thing to another and the curious presence of bodies in a space that are sanitized from potential contamination come to mind. That is also how I begin to think about the other interlopers and interlocutors that occupy the exhibition's peripheries and centers in equal measure: a fragrance orchestrated by Dora Budor; Charles Gaines's *Falling Rock* (2000) unexpectedly breaking through a sheet of glass; a fantastical tree carved from polyurethane foam by Piero Gilardi; a heat-sensitive bench, conceived by Cooper Jacoby and outfitted with a thermostat that answers the question "How will I survive?"; Jules Gimbrone and Micah Silver's research into Schlieren imaging; Morag Keil's pneumatic tube system processing the architecture's biological matter. This list encompasses some of the contributions being pursued as *Lifes* enters into its final planning stages. The end results are still cohering and their meanings in relation to others are still in formation. Meanwhile, as of now, Adania Shibli's "An Aesthetic Misunderstanding or the wind that did not see the grass that did not hear its whistle" lives solely in the pages of this catalogue, expressing a formal incompatibility with the galleries of the museum. The exhibition will include more works than are discussed here, but writing about them as if they were finished and discrete units would deceive the project as a whole and undermine the potency of their assembly. *Lifes* is the result of compression, its shape will be determined by the composite of voices and intermediaries that have been brought into its orbit to work within the context of the museum.

In *Temple of the Scapegoat: Opera Stories*, author and filmmaker Alexander Kluge conjures the power of voice: "In the twentieth century the Great Singing Machines were developed, mainly in the academies of the two superpowers. A voice singing with total commitment was capable of rupturing eardrums, even utterly destroying the brain by deploying resonance at short range. A resolute voice can kill."[19] Kluge describes the voice as a weaponized lifeform inherited from the theatrical stage. Kluge's words, like those of the other discursive helpers that surround the exhibition, pass through me and onto the pages of

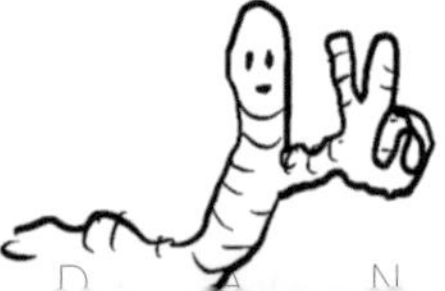

this publication. I teleport between their historical positions, their research interests, and the conversations happening in real time with the contributors to this overall project. This is a framework for understanding what Enwezor characterized as the *state of things*. It is also what one might call the lived condition known as *Lifes*.

Notes

1. Jessye Norman, *Stand Up Straight and Sing!* (Boston: Mariner Books, 2014), 49–50.
2. Vaslav Nijinsky, *The Diary of Vaslav Nijinsky*, ed. Joan Acocella (New York: Farrar, Straus and Giroux, 1999), 110.
3. Nijinsky, *The Diary of Vaslav Nijinsky*, 127.
4. Marie Rambert, quoted in *The Search for Nijinsky's Rite of Spring*, dir. Judy Kinberg, 1989, https://www.youtube.com/watch?v=ROIqerRbM-c.
5. For a discussion of the debates surrounding Wagner, including critiques by Friedrich Nietzsche, Theodor Adorno, and Bertolt Brecht, see Juliet Koss, "Invisible Wagner," *Modernism after Wagner* (Minneapolis: University of Minnesota Press, 2010), 245–73.
6. Annette Michelson, "'Where Is Your Rupture?' Mass Culture and the *Gesamtkunstwerk*," *October* 56 (Spring 1991): 43.
7. Writing in 1983, on the occasion of Harald Szeeman's exhibition *Der Hang zum Gesamtkunstwerk* (The tendency toward the total work of art) at Kunsthaus Zurich, Italian curator and critic Germano Celant warns of an apparent anti-historicism that risks submitting to the mystique of the total work of art. See Germano Celant, "Der Hang zum Gesamtkunstwerk," *Artforum* 56 (September 1983). The exhibition and Szeeman's legacy loom large in the history of exhibitions. Curator Hans Ulrich Obrist has recounted the significance of *Der Hang zum Gesamtkunstwerk* on his curatorial approach, citing his forty-one visits to the exhibition when he was a teenager. Obrist's indebtedness to Szeeman and Diaghilev is recounted in almost any interview or article of press that takes the curator as its subject. See Hans Ulrich Obrist, quoted in Paul Holdengraber, "The Master Interviewer," *Surface* (September 28, 2016), https://surfacemag.com/articles/hansulrich.
8. Okwui Enwezor, "The Akhand Path: To Read Without Stopping," *56th International Art Exhibition: All the World's Futures* (Venice, Italy: Fondazione La Biennale di Venezia, 2015), 210.
9. It is reported that, in the runup to the company's Paris debut in 1909, Diaghilev's confidant Walter Nouvel dismissed the musical accompaniment for the ballet *Cléopâtra* as a mediocre "salade russe." See Sjeng Scheijen, *Diaghilev: A Life* (New York: Oxford University Press, 2009), 176.

10. Jacques Rancière, *Aisthesis: Scenes from the Aesthetic Regime of Art* (Brooklyn, NY: Verso, 2019), xi.
11. Rancière, *Aisthesis*, 61.
12. Daisy Hildyard, *The Second Body* (London: Fitzcarraldo Editions, 2017), 57.
13. Lawrence D. "Butch" Morris, "Introduction to the Conduction Lexicon," *The Art of Conduction: A Conduction Workbook*, ed. Daniela Veronesi (New York: Karma, 2017), 43.
14. Anna Lowenhaupt Tsing, *The Mushroom at the End of the World* (Princeton, NJ: Princeton University Press, 2015), 22–24.
15. Wayne Koestenbaum, *The Queen's Throat* (Boston: Da Capo Press, 2001), 144.
16. Silvia Rivera Cusicanqui, *Ch'ixinakax utxiwa: On Practices and Discourses of Decolonization* (Medford, MA: Polity Press, 2020), 54–55.
17. Mattilda Bernstein Sycamore, *The Freezer Door* (South Pasadena, CA: Semiotext(e), 2020), 129.
18. Fred Moten, *Black and Blur* (Durham, NC: Duke University Press, 2017), 202.
19. Alexander Kluge, *Temple of the Scapegoat: Opera Stories* (New York: New Directions Publishing, 2018), 69.

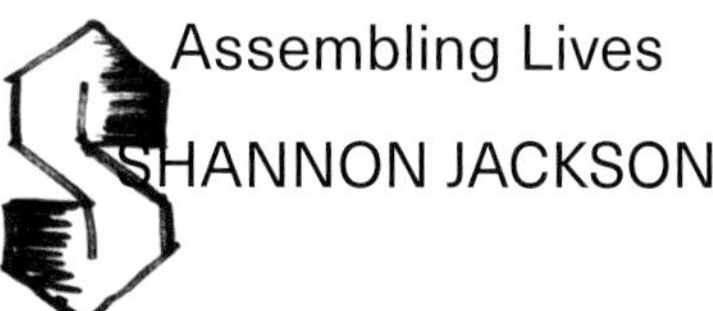

Assembling Lives

SHANNON JACKSON

Starting in the Middle

Assemblage is a potent word these days—and in past days. It recalls the political conception of the assembly as a vehicle of democratic governance. It recalls the artistic history of assemblage as an extended collage and juxtaposition of, to quote the *Oxford English Dictionary*, "miscellaneous parts." It could recall the industrial history of the assembly line in the production of commodities, asking how that association squares with our (and the museum's) postindustrial moment of service provision. It might even recall the archeological conception of assembly, the delimited excavation space where past creatures left fossilized remnants as indexes of past lives to those living (and studying them) now. With all of these associations in the back of one's mind, an ecological association of assemblage certainly lies front of mind. From Gilles Deleuze and Brian Massumi to a host of thinkers associated with contemporary climate theory, affect theory, and new materialisms, *assemblage* is a resonant term for characterizing relationships amongst systems, non-volitional agencies, and sentient beings, including those that used to be called humans. Its resonance has an urgent ring as some of those used-to-be-called-humans think about how to write, how to curate, how to make art, and how to live a life in a landscape of erosion.

On Mixing Lifes and Liveness

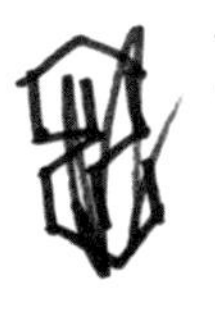

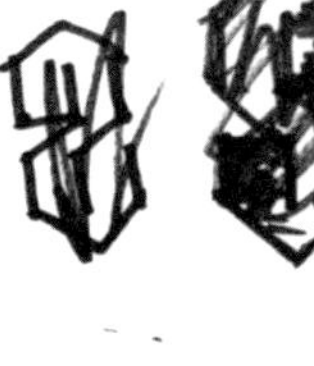

In art contexts and in various intellectual contexts, ideas of assemblage might also invite a discourse of "interdisciplinarity," whatever we think we mean by that term. In such contexts, disciplines of practice and disciplines of knowledge making find themselves combined, poached, appropriated, hybridized, reinvented, and mixed in various assemblages. Assemblage might indeed require interdisciplinary play. But perhaps interdisciplinary play is a play that has become old, or old enough to prompt

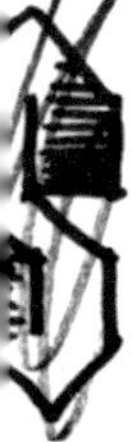

many of us to ask for something else. But before we get too hasty, let's reflect on what it is, including those movements in modernist ballet and opera oft-celebrated for their proto-interdisciplinarity.

We could start with the Ballets Russes. Propelled by its impresario, Sergei Diaghilev, in the early twentieth century, this itinerant dance company is known for the power of its artistic mixtures. From ballet's proscenium stages, the company became a moving platform of experimentation, one that joined the embodied feats of the virtuosic dancers with sonic accompaniments and spectacular sets created by composers, visual artists, and designers: Claude Debussy, Igor Stravinsky, Vasily Kandinsky, Pablo Picasso, Henri Matisse, Coco Chanel, and more. The Ballets Russes mixed the disciplines of dance, painting, music, and design in novel combinations, energizing its own aesthetic while providing a stage—literally—and a marketing platform—implicitly—for then contemporaneous artists. Famously, the Ballets Russes never performed in Russia; indeed, its generative moment came in France, when Diaghilev was asked to create an exhibition of Russian art at the Petit Palais in Paris. Aware that he would never be a great artist, this scion of a vodka distillery realized that he could convene great artists and do a better job mining the histories of Russian aesthetics—even celebrating the motifs of its folklore—when they were displaced from their country of origin. Diaghilev's transnational displacement allowed the forms to flourish, or, at the very least, Russian contours and aesthetic innovation became visible when placed within an unfamiliar context. Whether or not we call that transnational effect strategic or un-strategic, the interplay of the Ballets Russes contains a lesson about the interplay of interdisciplinarity, even as it anticipated some of the opportunities and blind spots of a globalizing art world. As most contemporary scholars will tell you, it is in moving a discipline from its epistemological origin into the home of another that we become most keenly attuned to the characteristics of the former. Its vocabulary is estranged; its methods are de-normalized; its reality principles become specific and particular rather than normal and habitual. The norms and habits of their home country become newly visible when migrants enter a new host country.

Whether entering a new nation or experimenting in someone else's professional field, that "interdisciplinary" awareness is both productive and destabilizing. This is to say that there is a kind of revelation here when travel between home and host countries cuts across the disciplines of the arts. The Ballets Russes combined dance, painting, music, and design; a contemporary iteration of this assemblage might combine other art forms—choreographers and composers, theater directors and dramaturgs, alongside the more recent designations performance, video, and installation artists. In that line up, one might notice a preponderance of artists hailing from the so-called "live" performing arts. An updating of the Ballets Russes' working methodologies today might propose cross-art conversation and collaboration, another play about interplay, and another chance for the techniques, contours, habits, and blind spots of different art forms to become visible to each other. And audible to each other. As much as an interdisciplinary discourse might celebrate the jostling and unsettling of separate worlds and practices, these occasions might also reveal the foundationally inseparate nature of the arts, as well as the foundationally unseparated nature of all components of the life world. The museum has always depended upon the tacit choreographies and sonic prescriptions of the gallery space. Theater needs the poet and the architect and the painter. Dance, too. And on and on. The normalization and naturalization of these inter-art collaborations keep their participants from noticing them and recognizing the importance of the arts ecology that they share.

On Receiving Mixture

What, then, is the role of viewers in experimental curatorial processes that mix art forms and, by extension, modes of reception? If we were being true to a spirit of assemblage and experimentation, perhaps we should have started with them. Imagine viewers adopting a stance on art that has yet to be generated. However challenging such a concept might be technically and institutionally, its conceptual implications move us into slightly different philosophical territory. The long arc of twentieth- and twenty-first-century experimental art might well be reframed as a fitful and contradictory process of avowing and disavowing the role of the receiver in the production of the artwork. If that long arc can also be reframed as a fitful and contradictory process of welcoming and rejecting inter-art collaboration—from the *Gesamtkunstwerk* (total work of art) through Dada and surrealism, from the Ballets Russes to Happenings to new genres to multimedia to Whatever It Is That We Think We Are Doing Now—then one would think that any evocation of artistic mixture has to contend with the viewer and the various ways that the arts try to address her—indirectly, directly, or through broken fourth walls.

But there again, if we try to join the topic of reception to the topic of interdisciplinary arts, we first have to contend with the different ways that different art forms name this receiver: the viewer, the beholder, the listener, the spectator, and the audience member, along with the more contemporary or institutional associations, such as the visitor, the user, the member, the collaborator, the neighbor, or the participant of relational aesthetics (who, by the by, differs in stance and behavior from the participant of participatory theater). Indeed, the metaphor of breaking the fourth wall comes from theater, a certain tradition of theater that takes place on a proscenium stage, where bodies perform dramatic dialogue in front of an audience that they pretend is not there. Does a painting pretend that the audience isn't there? Well, yes, one can suppose it does, and a number of modernist art critics wanted it so. A modernist painting could, theoretically, criticize itself without depending upon a receiver. Of course, it is exactly the flawed assumption that art could exist independently of its reception that art movements that preceded and followed modernism sought to expose. And yet, the fourth wall assumed the prior existence of a certain kind of wall and a certain kind of theatrical pretending. It requires an inter-art imagination to spy a link between the exposure of fourth walls on a proscenium stage and the exposure of dry-walled walls in the gallery. It means seeing a link between, say, something like Bertolt Brecht's exposures and the minimalist and post-minimalist exposures of Institutional Critique. Since I've tried to foreground that link in other writings, I won't repeat the line of thought here. But I do think it's worth noting those moments when the deployment of a distinct cross-arts aesthetic propelled viewer self-consciousness.

Indeed, for Brecht's epic theater, this intermedia mixture had to have a specific character. Brecht distinguished his theatrical practice from that of Richard Wagner, the opera innovator who famously elaborated the *Gesamtkunstwerk* as a fusion of aesthetic elements in a "Drama" form that celebrated "Feeling." Said Wagner: "Only in the most perfect artwork therefore, in the Drama, can the insight of the experienced one impart itself with full success; and for the very reason that, through employment of every artistic expressional-faculty of man, the poet's aim is in Drama the most completely carried from the Understanding to the Feeling."[1] For Brecht, however, this focus on fusion and on feeling produced an uncritical, de-politicized theater, one whose "culinary effects" of entertainment, pleasure, and consumption he denounced. For Brecht, critical reflection could only occur in a theater where there was an emphatic separation of the elements. In this separation and mutual de-familiarization of dance, music, poetry, and painting, the politically engaged consciousness of an epic theater spectator could blossom:

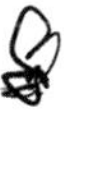

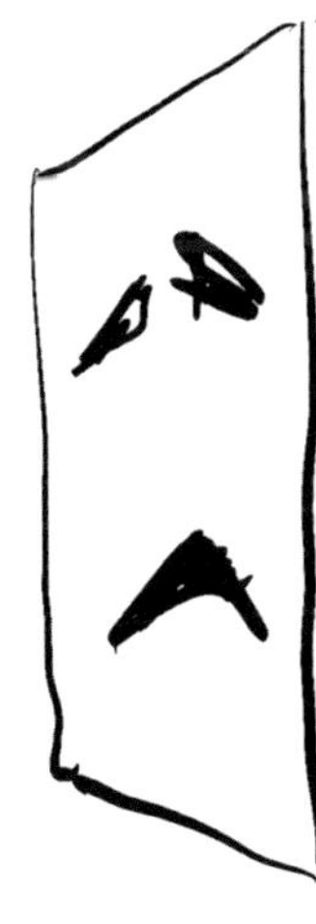

> When the epic theatre's methods begin to penetrate the opera, the first result is a radical *separation of the elements.* The great struggle for supremacy between words, music, and production—which always brings up the question "which is the pretext for what?": is the music the pretext for the events on the stage, or are these the pretext for the music? etc.—can simply be bypassed by radically separating the elements. So long as the expression "Gesamtkunstwerk" (or "integrated work of art") means that the integration is a muddle, so long as the arts are supposed to be "fused" together, the various elements will all be equally degraded. . . . The process of fusion extends to the spectator, who gets thrown into the melting pot too and becomes a passive (suffering) part of the total work of art. Witchcraft of this sort must of course be fought against. . . . *Words, music, and setting must become more independent of one another.*[2]

Receivers should see, hear, and feel that inter-art collaboration, to be aware of the separation amongst "words, music, and set" (or installation), rather than the aesthetic event being allowed to devolve into the fused, ecstatic oblivion of culinary art and consumptive spectatorship. If now, in the twenty-first century, a curatorial assemblage seeks to gather artistic disciplines without asking them to function according to their respective bounds, Brecht might ask where or whether a critical consciousness in the viewer will arise.

Inhospitality and Interpellation

Indeed, what is culinary and what is critical for us now? The lines between them might already be blurred, along with divisions amongst the arts, along with divisions amongst species and systems, along with divisions between maker and spectator. What effects will ensue? And what affects? Isn't the twenty-first-century openness to participatory genres and relational media a generous and hospitable act? The art sees you and welcomes you. The art does not want to exist before you do; it doesn't make its entrance before you make yours.

Of course, it turns out that many viewers appreciate the comfort of following familiar rules and being allowed to enter spaces that affirm what they tacitly already know. The best form of hospitality is the one that you don't notice, after all, like ideology. Those of us who admiringly chronicle the history of the so-called avant-garde record these moments of spectatorial shock and disorientation, hoping that viewers get over it, that they come to realize that a little bit of edgy inhospitality is actually good for them. Perhaps they can wash it down with a shot of Diaghilevian vodka.

Amid this morass of rules and affects, of habits that numb and habits that comfort, it might be worth trying to think from all interdisciplinary angles simultaneously. It might be worth recognizing that the art historical preoccupation with the viewer is part of a longer philosophical history whose contours one can mine without ever breaking free. If I bring in a few chestnuts from the field of performance studies, we can recall the rhetorical strain of performativity theory. That strain has certainly found a purchase in contemporary art criticism that is trying to grapple with Whatever It Is That We Think We Are Doing Now. In fact, the recent revision of performativity theory was part of a broader effort to understand the complexities of subject formation, a project that questioned the assumption that self-making was essentially a voluntary operation, regulated only by the exercise of internal will. Many recent thinkers, such as Michel Foucault, Jacques Derrida, and Judith Butler, have excavated a history of critical philosophy to mount alternative conceptions, frames that take seriously the degree to which social circumstances in fact produce our internal perception of a voluntary will, often with particular ideological effects.[3] It was in such a context that the notion of the "performative" was revived, this time to tease out the implications of the constitutive power of language that lies at the center of J. L. Austin's excavation in *How to Do Things with Words*. Indeed, for many recent theorists, it is most important to consider the degree to which the primary "doing" of the performative is the ideological constitution of the doer herself.

To ground a complex notion, let's look at one famous example of dramatized recursion. Louis Althusser's *Ideology and Ideological State Apparatuses* is a key text in this conversation, particularly for his vocabulary of "hailing" and "interpellation" and for the example he used to describe how we participate in our own ideological formation:

> That very precise operation which I have called *interpellation* or hailing . . . can be imagined along the lines of the most commonplace everyday police (or other) hailing: "Hey, you there!" Assuming that the theoretical scene I have imagined takes place in the street, the hailed individual will turn round. By this mere one hundred and eighty degree physical conversion, he becomes a *subject*. Why? Because he has recognized that the hail was "really" addressed to him, and that "it was *really him* who was hailed" (and not someone else). Experience shows that the practical telecommunication of hailing is such that they hardly ever miss their man: verbal call or whistle, the one hailed always recognizes that it is really him who is being hailed.[3]

Althusser's teachable example proved fruitful for many subsequent conversations in critical theory. It temporarily anthropomorphized ideology as a cop whose performative utterance sought an addressee; moreover, it was through one physically and psychically allowing oneself *to be addressed* that ideology did its work. That famous "turn" was a form of uptake that ensured the felicitousness of ideology's performative reach. Moreover, Althusser was keen to note that the process of address and uptake had a temporal coincidence: "Naturally for the convenience and clarity of my little theoretical theater I have had to present things in the form of a sequence, with a before and an after, and thus in the form of a temporal succession. . . . But in reality these things happen without any succession. The existence of ideology and the hailing or interpellation of individuals as subjects are one and the same thing."[4] Althusser thus posited interpellation *of* subjects *by* ideology as itself a recursive process, as "one and the same thing." Joining an Austinian language with an Althusserian one, Judith Butler attempts to tease out a degree of variability in the process of hailing: "As Althusser himself insists, this performative effort of naming can only attempt to bring its addressee into being; there is always the risk of a certain misrecognition. If one misrecognizes that effort to produce the subject, the production itself falters. The one who is hailed may fail to hear, misread the call, turn the other way, answer to another name, insist on not being addressed that way."[5] At the same time, if misfire or misrecognition is possible, it still occurs within a recursive structure that both constrains and enables the subjects it made. Oddly enough, it seems that we are caught between the ideological incorporation of utter misunderstanding and the peculiar productivity of fleeting misrecognition. Perhaps inhabiting new assemblages means relinquishing a volitional notion of critical consciousness in the receiver, encouraging us instead to inhabit this in-between.

The Genre of Assemblage

Having reflected upon how and whether a philosophical genealogy of performativity might bear upon the performative assemblages of our current moment, we might further explore whether this is a new kind of blurring of genres—or a new genre altogether. Such a question, of course, might presume to place human invention at its base. It might presume to foreground and re-center an artist's innovation or a critic's analytic perception in deciding upon the bounds of this genre-in-the-making. Indeed, a proposition along these lines lies at the center of a paradoxical in-between, in that it still commissions those of us who used to be called humans to enter its process. However, we can also say that, by inverting or upending or redirecting our processes, any such utilization of us so-called humans is also de-centering anything that might be called artistic or critical volition, much less critical or artistic intention. That de-centering chimes with the sensibilities of other contemporary assemblages, displacing the human from the center of the lifeworld and into a dispersion of generative forces, materials, and systems.

Before breaking from the old play of genre, however, we might remind ourselves, once again, what it is. We can also remind ourselves that even the word *genre* functions differently in different art forms. The *genre* of genre painting carries a different association than those attached to the word in dance, music, theater, and film. Indeed, probably the most influential and precise elaboration of genre occurred in literature. Within Western classical literary theory, we have supposedly inherited a triad of literary forms: the epic, the lyric, and the dramatic. If you believe Gérard Genette, this "classical" genre triad was an invention of the Romantic period.[6] At the same time, it is interesting to think about how this triad shifts an axis of comparison, while revealing more heterogeneity within the category of "writing" or "literature" in our inter-art conversation. Recall the lyric's association with first-person expression and its link to a form of a personal revelation. Recall the epic's association with narrative, often a third-person narrative that recounts and contains the capacity to traverse identifications and time periods. From this angle of vision, drama comes forward most specifically as a dialogic genre based in mimetic substitution, where actors stand in for characters who take part in a particular form of structured exchange. Or, as Genette would say, where the artist speaks through characters who appear to speak for themselves. By delineating amongst temporal poetic genres, such as the lyric, the dramatic, and the epic, we might find ourselves wondering if different classic genres offer more traction for understanding the cross-art experimentation of today. In fact, my sense is that much of what now passes for innovation in event-based, relational, process, and performance art is more often linked to the lyric or the epic than it is to the dramatic. Any such acknowledgment of this distinction might eventually lead to these old literary genres both receiving and feeding new life in an ecological assembly.

The ambiguities and system failures of our current moment challenge us to occupy the provisionally productive space of assemblage. It is a space where energies come unbidden, where tacit systems are exposed, where new connections are revealed to have been there all along. As such, the processes of assembling art also ride with the processes of living in all its confusion, buoyancy, and unexpected kinship. To reassemble the arts—separately and collectively, affectively and critically—gives us a vehicle for differently experiencing our lives. It gives us a fragile, temporary frame for apprehending whatever it is that we think we are enduring now.

Notes

1. Richard Wagner, *Opera and Drama* (first published in 1851) (Lincoln: University of Nebraska Press, 1995), 208.
2. Bertolt Brecht, "Modern Theater Is the Epic Theater," *Brecht on Theater: The Development of an Aesthetic*, ed. and trans. John Willett (New York: Hill & Wang, 1977), 37–38. Italics added for emphasis.
3. Louis Althusser, "Ideology and Ideological State Apparatuses," *Lenin and Philosophy and Other Essays* (New York: New York University Press, 2001), 162–63.
4. Althusser, "Ideology and Ideological State Apparatuses," 162–63.
5. Judith Butler, "Subjection, Resistance, Resignification: Between Freud and Foucault," *The Psychic Life of Power: Theories in Subjection* (Stanford, CA: Stanford University Press, 1997), 95.
6. See Gérard Genette, *The Architext: Modern Genre Theory*, ed. David Duff (New York: Longman, 2000).

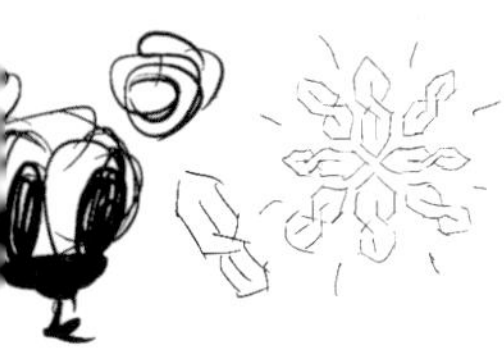

Black Music as Curation

GREG TATE

If, as composer and 2020 National Endowment for the Arts Jazz Master Henry Threadgill advocates, we begin to tag the entire history of recorded Black music as a field saturated with sound designers engaged in making sound art—and dispense with the plethora of idiomatic commercial markers the world knows, such as jazz, blues, hip-hop, funk, R&B, soul—then we unveil the curatorial instincts and critical practices that have always operated across the spectrum of musics we designate as Black in origin, evolution, execution, and experimentation.

The flotilla of archival box sets dedicated to extraordinary artists of note—James Brown, Little Richard, Aretha Franklin, Miles Davis, Thelonious Monk—already compels us to reimagine their decades-deep bodies of sound design work as curatorial in nature. The visual, literary, and choreographic elements working in representational tandem with their sonic properties demand we reexamine the work from multiple aesthetic perspectives.

From the vast photographic evidence we possess, Miles Davis certainly saw not only his music but also his very bespoke self as a modernist art object. In 1970s Washington, DC (where this writer was raised), it became a running joke that the question asked of attendees of his concerts on the morning after wasn't "What did he play?" but rather "What was he wearing?"

James Brown, who never spoke much about his music, declared, "As long as a man has hair and teeth, he has everything." In an even more meta comment about his work, Brown observed, "I make music for the ugly man." Thelonious Monk's composition title "Ugly Beauty" could be taken as the expression of an artistic prescription and imperative for Monk's entire canon. Monk drew inspiration from his conversations with artist Piet Mondrian, who was a frequent habitue of the Harlem club Minton's in the 1940s, where Monk and his compatriots workshopped the music we call bebop. Apparently, a

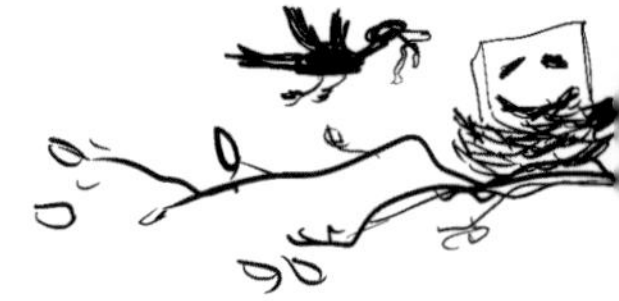

photograph of Billie Holiday on the ceiling of Monk's bedroom kept him creatively charged during the many years he spent at home, when a ban on musicians accused of drug possession prevented him from playing in New York clubs.

In 2008, Christie's auctioned the James Brown Collection. Among the 360 items was Brown's array of multicolored, torso-revealing jumpsuits, which were embroidered and emblazoned with the word *SEX*—costumes befitting a performer who described himself in song (and terpsichore) as a "sex machine." The varied auctioned objects, which also included musical instruments, easy chairs, jewelry, and platform shoes, would have made for a spectacular Whitney Biennial installation.

Certainly, the stage and album-cover presentation of Miles Davis's 1970s electronic epoch qualified as an intentionally curated affair. Eye-popping artwork by Abdul Mati Klarwein, Corky McCoy, and the Japanese collagist Tadanori Yokoo adorned the jackets of his pivotal releases of this era. On stage, the mid-seventies band was flanked by speaker columns that displayed the tricolored Black Liberation flag. Every musician had an immaculate Afro, and the dress code encompassed silk scarves, Afrocentric dashikis, bell-bottom pants, and tight-knit shirts. When viewing the YouTube videos of Miles Davis Group performances from those years, you can't not see that Davis was presenting an arrangement of kinetic sculpture as much as a blistering, future-leaning musical affair. Davis, of course, drew much from the carnivalesque music and innovative fashions of Jimi Hendrix, whose albums brought cinematic soundscapes to the fore, and Sly Stone, who curated biracial and mixed gender ensembles that beat out the exploitation of human diversity by United Colors of Benetton ads by three decades.

Of course, no Black sound designer had been leaning into the future with more visionary curatorial verve since the 1950s than Sun Ra and His Myth Science Arkestra. Like Davis, the entity known as Sun Ra left behind a photographic and filmed record that makes clear that he saw himself as a self-fashioned art object, and he outfitted his musicians in mandatory Astro Black costuming for the stage. Every performance of Ra and

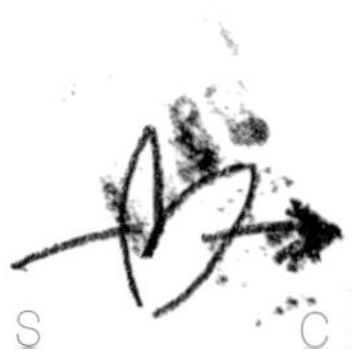

the Arkestra was mythopoeic in sweep and flair, offering the gifts of as many as twenty virtuosic players, music that invoked antiquity and futurity, and lyrics and lectures that explored Ra's philosophy. Topics included his birth on Saturn, "The Nubians of Plutonia," his desire for Black folk to "transmolecularize" to alternate planes of existence, "alternate destines," "fate in a pleasant mood," and "pictures of infinity." Ra also declared that the United States is not a democracy but rather a mythocracy held together by a gaggle of potent but fragile symbols of white nationalism—The Flag, The Anthem, The Constitution, The Pentagon, The Superbowl—that we've watched wither in our own time. The violent attempted coup at the United States Capitol Building on January 6, 2021, demonstrated to what degree MAGA devotees have replaced the myths of democracy with an ideology of anarchy and demonology.

Ra believed that Black folk have the potential to craft and adopt a mythocracy of their own choosing and design. George Clinton's Parliament-Funkadelic collective appears to have answered Ra's call when it dropped a bevy of concept albums in the 1970s. Thematically, musically, and visually, the albums—*Maggot Brain, Cosmic Slop, Mothership Connection, Funkentelechy vs. the Placebo Syndrome, The Clones of Dr. Funkenstein, The Motor Booty Affair, One Nation Under a Groove, The Brides of Dr. Funkenstein, The Electric Spanking of War Babies, Atomic Dog, R&B Skeletons in the Closet*, etc.—proposed and mass-popularized a slew of "altered destines," imaginaries and mythocracies for the Black community.

Within all of these albums are cautionary and conspiratorial readings of American capitalism and consumerism as hidden sinister and weaponized manipulations of We the People via communications technology and media. Clinton evolved his P-Funk Army into a set of codebreakers engaged in overcoming "urge overkill, or the pimping of the pleasure principle." The critique extended to the hypocrisy and racial disparities of the so-called war on drugs (see the track "U.S. Custom Coast Guard Dope Dog"). Their productions also extended escapist routes to outer space and Atlantis, which were metaphors for

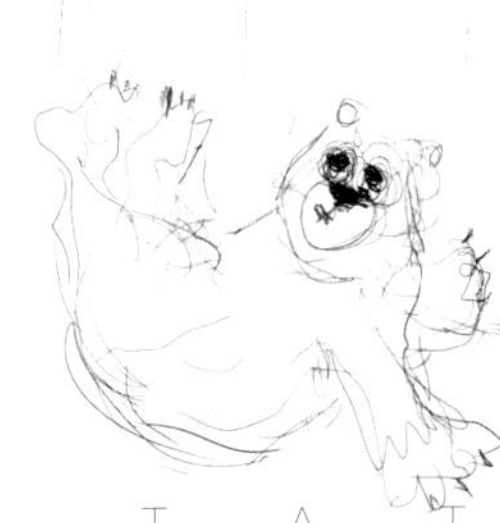

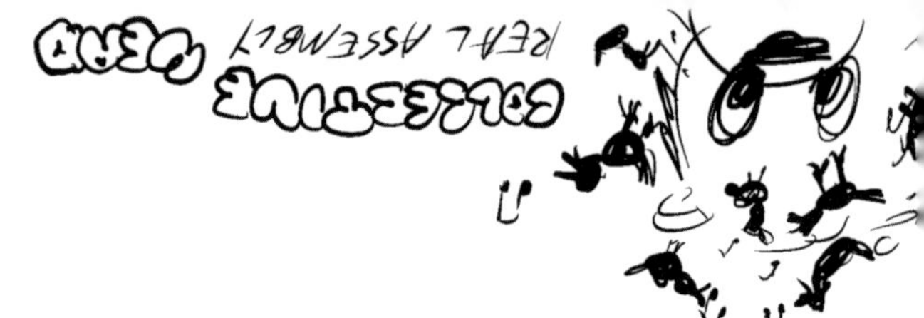

self-possessed Black bodies finding liberation through movement. "The rhythm of vision is a dancer," Clinton observes on *Motor Booty Affair* ("where we'll be going underwater and not coming up for air"). He polemically fortifies the action with this belief: "With the rhythm it takes to dance through what we have to live through . . . you can dance underwater and not get wet."

These Afro-aquatic tangents were picked up by Drexciya, the Detroit techno sound artists Gerald Donald and James Stinson. In the mid-eighties, the duo imagineered a full-blown mythos called Drexciya—a high-tech militarized Black underwater civilization founded by the spawn of pregnant African women who'd thrown themselves from slave ships into the Atlantic during the Middle Passage. The range of Drexciya productions includes vinyl releases, maps, manifestoes, paintings, and ideograms, and their work inspired a host of other sound designers and visual artists, such as Ellen Gallagher and Ayana Vellissia Jackson, who globally proliferate Drexciya's ideations in the twenty-first century.

In the 1980s, post-graffiti artists Lady Pink, Futura, Fab Five Freddy, Rammellzee, and Jean-Michel Basquiat embodied linkages between the gallery, the street, the stage, the video clip, and the recording studio, presciently covering a great, fantastical distance. Rammellzee was a pivotal figure who projected his body and soul into the world as a self-curated Black art object, battle-suit creator, performer, and theorizer of Black art as cultural warfare. He was a significant curatorial theorist, with his neo-art-historical framing of 1970s subway writing as "Ikonoklast Panzerism" and "Gothic Futurism." He symbolically mobilized these theoretical operations against the "biologically diseased and colonizing language systems of Western Civilization 101."

The reframing of ostensibly canonical Black music avatars as sound designers can also be extended back to the nineteenth and early twentieth centuries, for example in ragtime inventor Scott Joplin's hoodoo-centered opera *Treemonisha* (1911). Joplin performed an ingenious, audacious, and innovative remix of European operatic form, which he bent to his syncopated variations and used to tell an epic story steeped in mystical non-Christian Black American folklore. Early jazz band leader James Reese Europe and his Clef Club Orchestra made their one-hundred-piece symphony debut at Carnegie Hall in 1912 with a presentation that was curated as much visually as musically—as demonstrated by the multiple non-performing figures onstage who were there solely as window dressing.

Other foundational, influential, and enduring figures of curation and audiovisual performance and sound design in Black popular music history would have to include Duke Ellington, in his "jungle music" phase at the Cotton Club; Bessie Smith; Billie Holiday; Howling Wolf; Chuck Berry; Bo Diddley; Fela Kuti, with his architectonic Afrika Shrine and twenty-seven bootylicious dervish dancing wives; Bob Marley's fusion of Rasta visuality, iconography, and reggae music; and, of course, Little Richard, in all his audacious pancaked, bouffanted, and lipsticked glory long before queering the American pop-scape was safe for men of any color.

Important to remember in this recasting is that all of the Black sound artists whose projects were fomented in Jim Crow America were invisible as human beings, let alone as hyper-imaginative multidisciplinary sound artists, barred as their brilliance was from cinema and television, the previous century's dominant mediums of social representation. To paraphrase what one mentor to this writer, Billy Quinn, said in the late 1970s, any people not in major media in the twentieth century could be said not to exist at all. The compensatory self-empowerment of these sound-design projects and practices—their nonstop opposition to the invisibility wars mounted against BIPOC folk by white mass media (and the twentieth century's apartheid-oriented white art world)—cannot be overstated. Visionary Black musicians made sound and stage spectacle their cinema alternative in ways that challenged, confronted, and out-glamoured the stereotypes Black listeners, dancers, and spectators were getting from Hollywood.

The totality of this historic plenitude of Black audiovisual imaginaries, mythos, and *Gesamtkunstwerk* is now embraced

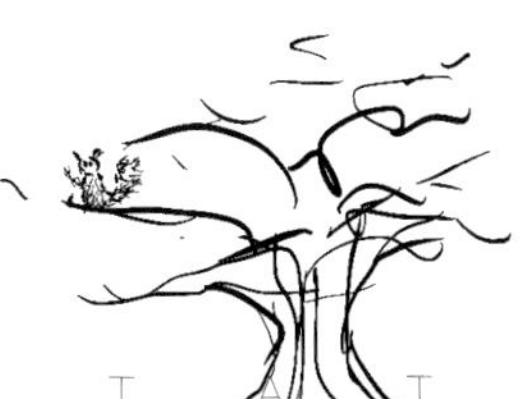

by the developing pedagogies, scholarship, and disciplines of Afrofuturism (the rhythm and projection of Afrocentric vision and imagineering—prophetic, aesthetic, speculative, and scientific—throughout the spectrum of humanity's creative disciplines) and Afrosurrealism (the language of Black dreamscapes). The curatorial potential of both epistemologies shall certainly come into wider recognition and provenance as vital cultural resources and radical criticalities before the half mark of this century.

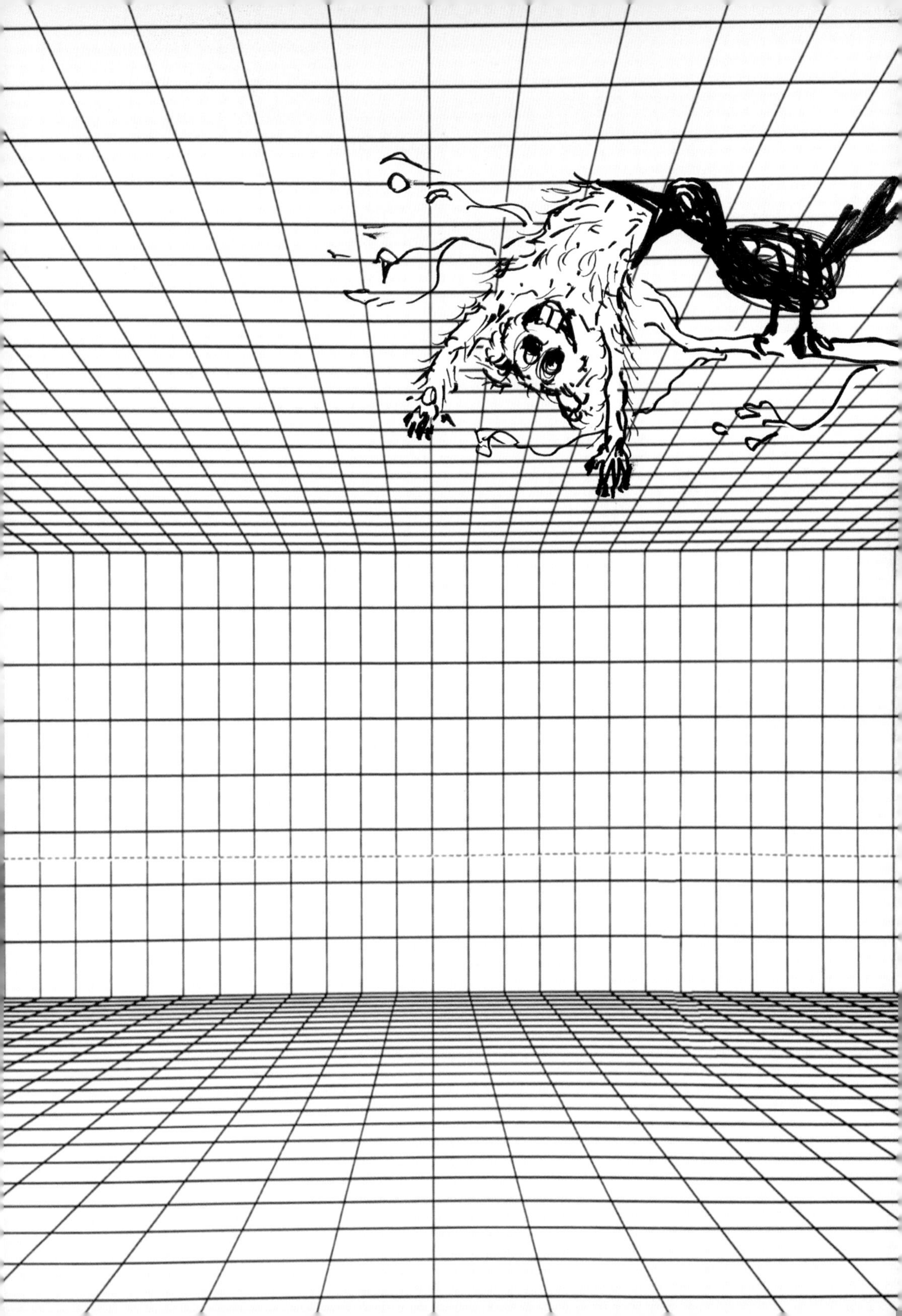

Stealing Colors

FAHIM AMIR

For me, colors are like animals.

Some of them have no history, others have too much.

In Italian, a color without a name is referred to as *color cane che fugge*—literally, the color of a dog that flees—for example, if someone buys themselves a sweater and their relatives can't figure out what color it is. It's neither fish nor fowl. In Portuguese, it's called *cor de burro quando foge*, the color of a donkey that flees.

An Abbreviated Account of *Lifes*

Edited and compiled by Nicholas Barlow

The following is a partial account of conversations and correspondence between contributors to *Lifes* in the months leading up to the publication's print deadline. The text has been edited for length and clarity; crossed out passages indicate false starts and ideas that were abandoned.

sher Hartman: I have a process of writing r a long time and then kind of sculpting e piece, picking aspects of the piece that I ink are vibrant and then working on those arts to put them into some shape.

A lot of the writing is inspired by living L.A. since 1977, largely on the edges of nything that could be considered classic os Angeles, but instead in a mix of people ho have dual lives: security guards, beeper alespeople, the Coffee Bean & Tea Leaf omedians, healthy porn stars, drifters, uman-animal people, all with some hidden rce or ability inside.

In part the piece is also inspired by egas cabaret, which perhaps doesn't just erge on the obscene but contains the ramped libidinal, visceral forces that inform ur politics, our drifting allegiances, our

Instead of making history, dogs and donkeys supposedly follow instincts and reflexes. They serve purposes: those of humans, of genes, of evolution, of ecosystems. In short, they dwell in the realm of unfreedom. At least that's what philosophy says. What this kind of thinking actually means is: there is nowhere to run, at least nowhere you'd want to follow the animals. The color of an animal that is fleeing is less than nothing. For European thinking, the bodies of animals were as questionable as those of colors. But the thinker Julia Kristeva reminds us that color is bodily, as is the voice: "Colour is not zero meaning; it is excess meaning."[1]

Colors fade, colors are mortal. As the indeterminate color of things that change their appearance with the light. As mysterious pigments for painting, whose recipes were often secret, whose origin in plants, animals, and minerals usually remained doubtful, and which sometimes came from distant, nameless lands. As suspicious dyes of materials that were considered diabolical because mixing, stirring, and blending contravened the divine order in the Christian Middle Ages. Whoever did this as an occupation, like dyers or apothecaries, attracted mistrust. As did artists who still mixed their paints themselves. It is said of the painter Vincent van Gogh that he had a thing for eating yellow paint, because he thought the color of sunshine would make not only his paintings happy but himself as well.

partial analyses of life in a way that is, in m
usual manner, a container for the unsee
and the unsightly, i.e., the psychologicall
obscene.

Adam Linder: It's an opportunity to fli
our usual casting prerequisites. We don
need a group of high-caliber contemporar
dancers or a posse of actors. It seems tha
as the text and mise-en-scène evolve we
could build a hybrid cast around them—
one dancer, one actor, perhaps a Hamme
employee, and a porn star? Sounds like
a party.

I am also really enthused by thinking
about psychological undercurrents tha
bubble below "the structural." All human
are animals ~~and animal choreography i~~

~~omething I want to invest in more.~~

ram Moshayedi: He wants them to be, ~~I~~ ~~on't know, like, performance bodies. Like~~ ~~e wants them to really be a kind of more~~ ~~eal than~~ real people.

dam Linder: I have this deep intuition hat all the usual categories—durational, omentarily activated, timed, and looped— f live things occurring in the museum are bit stale.

There are themes about different gures (porn stars, museum guards, etc.) erforming themselves / performing their isembodied selves, psychic undertows of .A. vernaculars, and a kind of animalistic

From the moment of its birth, Western philosophy distrusted the semblance of colors. It wished to create what was immortal, but colors shimmer and fade. Colors change their color, so their stake in eternity is precarious. Perhaps that's why European philosophy always said: form before color. Ideal, imperishable forms, which dwell in the apparently colorless black and white of abstraction, promise immortality. The apparent eternity of form was cleansed of the transitoriness of the world. Yet it is impossible to think of any kind of form without color. Every form presupposes contrasting colors, according to the thinker Vilém Flusser, who lodges an objection against philosophy's obliviousness to color: "In fact we never see colorless forms—not even theoretically, with our 'mind's eye.' We see exclusively colors in various shapes, and that which we call 'form' is the border between distinct colors."[2]

But what is actually happening at the border between colors? Philosophy also dodges this question. Christian and Islamic philosophers have rarely gone beyond asking whether colors are part of light or part of the illuminated world. If they are part of light, then they share in divinity, in the Creator. If, on the other hand, colors are a part of things, then they are merely part of creation, doomed to extinction, mere illusion. Philosophy has never dealt very well with colors or taken them seriously. The same goes for animals. Animal : human = color : form?

emotional neediness around relations.

Rindon Johnson: ~~A "play" about som relationships between: Tide Pools, Californi Kelp Forests, Human Agents, Human Nor Agents, Rocks, Sand, and the Buffalo c~~ Catalina Island.

~~A ballet of some kind, a ballet that follow the etymology of the word *ballet*, which i to *jump around.*~~

~~In an ideal universe I would write a balle with the computer. First I would work wit a programmer to create a simple prograr using the language of my discursive helper and my previous books and writing to trai the program. I would then run the prograr to give me a seven-page enmeshing of th helpers. From there I'd translate (i.e., mak~~

~~egible) that scenario and overlay the likely haracters (see below) across it. I would do his five times, for five one acts to ultimately reate a programmed play all set within ome sort of house within the shoals.~~

dania Shibli: I would like to explore the elationship between words and images, ased on the observation made by Michel oucault on the word being blind and he image being deaf. So it will be an xploration of a contribution inspired by he relationship of deafness and blindness y which it refers to words and images but s not limited to that.

This will also relate to the idea of an xhibition where words and visuals have ften certain set paths as to how they can be

Having color seems to be a quality of that which is alive. Electromagnetic radiation has no color. Colors exist only where light beams are perceived as colors, and even more strongly where living beings generate colors. Colors play no role for star clusters or atoms. It is only in the dimension between them, for living things, that colors are associated with perception. Hence the overwhelming colorfulness of living beings, which, the philosopher Ludger Schwarte notes, surpasses the chemical and the physical.[3] The colorful field of flowers is an insect environment that reflects the insects themselves. Plants and their pollinators form an *Umwelt*, a milieu. They reflect each other, as in a shared dance. There is mutuality in the bitterness of a fruit and the being that perceives it. Colors are a way in which the world articulates itself as environment, as a surrounding world. Perception and world are not a chance acquaintanceship between things that are actually separate.[4] They depend on each other.

Still, in the theater of colors, it is often not clear to us which is the audience and which is the plot. The black and white of zebras' stripes repels flies. It took a very long time for this insight to get around. Who would have thought that the distinctive trait of these charismatic megafauna was aimed at creatures that had been considered relatively insignificant? Things do not seem much different among microfauna. There are eyeless roundworms living in our compost heap that consume bacteria. Some of these tiny worms are so afraid of blue-shimmering bacteria that they have learned to recognize blue without eyes or light-sensitive cells. Scientists speculate that it's possible that the worms bio-hacked protein bridges in their bodies to attain a sort of color vision.[5] All of this just because they detest the blue in the bacteria.

(catalogues with texts and images, caption and information about certain works, etc This will be part of the contribution, bu again not limited to it.

Aram Moshayedi: I keep returning to the ide of the presence of the viewer or visitor c whoever in the crafting of a museum space I am interested in the idea of the exhibitio as material, how artists can engage wit the material conditions of an exhibition t forge a new relationship to the question c viewership/audience.

There is an inherent degree c inhospitality that plays out in this scenario Perhaps even so much so that an exhibitio of this sort could be titled *Inhospitable*. Th viewer has been made aware they are th

oreign object in this space just as there
 a certain kind of foreignness that takes
laces between disciplinary approaches—
nese are never reconciled with one
nother, and the space of the contemporary
rt museum does what it can to absorb
ractices and identities and forms in the
ervice of representing a fleeting idea of
ne contemporary.

sher Hartman: All but one of the pieces
 have written for this work are direct
ddresses. In them, the speaker, the object,
 distanced from the viewer/participant/
nuseum visitor despite the urgent and
ften imploring manner in which the
peaker sometimes approaches the visitor.
he speaker is inhospitable and, in some

It is somewhat simpler for us humans: we possess three types of color-sensitive cells in our eyes, the so-called *cones*. Some cones react especially to short-wave blue light, others to medium-wave green light, and the rest to long-wave red light. Dogs, like many mammals, have only two types of cones, for blue and green. The canine rainbow is half as wide as the human one, and it has fewer colors. Most birds, fish, and reptiles have four types of cones. Their rainbow is wider than ours and has much more red. The pinnacle of color evolution is occupied by the mantis shrimp. They have twelve different color cones. They don't see more colors that those beings with seven or eight cones, but they recognize colors especially quickly.

In our earliest prehistory, we probably had four cones. When we started living nocturnally, that became two. When, like the other primates, we discovered the daytime for ourselves, we developed the third cone for a second time. Biologists say we developed color vision so we could distinguish better between various fruits and leaves. If that is true, trees and bushes were our first companions.

ways, "against" the viewer. The speaker ma occupy a corner, flit about, enter from th restroom, hurry toward the viewer, or stan still speaking to another who isn't there.

There are often slippages in time an place, attitude, in levels of hostility or seductio for example. None of the characters reall belong in the museum, and all may have som antipathy toward it. I'm interested in what performance in a museum may be taske with, the murkiness of the contract betwee performing artist and institution, what a bod is in that context, who a museum is for, an the impossibility of either party articulatin this contract with frankness.

Death, objecthood, celebrity, animatio porn, strapless rhinestone gowns, acrobatic grief and power, the museum as a "glowin cash register," as an unincorporated fortres s an inaccessible "thing" are some themes.

Rindon Johnson: *Inhospitable*. Yes. A good word to be thinking about while walking through the German countryside.

Who is this viewer anyway, and what sort of omnipotent impotence do they play, and what's the museum up to again?

I keep thinking about that yellow stringy cross piece at LACMA that kids run through and tired parents send them through so they can look at their phones and hit the vape. Like in that case there are four viewers: me, the kids, the parents, and the museum's bank account. We're all getting something out of it, and the only person who doesn't really catch that whiff is the kid viewer.

Absorb is a pretty good word, doing your

Now we can see more than a million colors. But distilling a certain, distinct color from this continuum is a different matter altogether, because the perception of a color always occurs in relation to other colors and shades. Our three types of cones reproduce not particular colors but blended color spectra of reddish, yellow-greenish, etc., which we perceive in relation to each other. We live in a universe of nuances and subtle transitions. We have to learn to recognize distinct colors; they are not simply there.

In the nineteenth century, the scholar William Gladstone was compelled, to his astonishment, to take note of this. He was so infatuated with the ancient poet Homer that he undertook to count the colors in Homer's epic poems—the wanderings of Odysseus and the battle for Troy. He was amazed to discover that the color blue was not mentioned a single time. The word *kuaneos*, which in later Greek meant *blue*, does appear in the poems, but for Homer it must have meant simply *dark*, for he uses it for neither the sky nor the sea, but only to describe Zeus's eyebrows, Hector's hair, or a dark cloud.[6] The sea is described in various ways. Homer's enigmatic formulation *wine-dark sea* has become famous, but one searches in vain for a sea of blue.[7]

best to absorb something sounds a bit lik sucking at it a lot. I like being bad at thing because I think it makes it all better. Coul the viewer be rendered shitty at looking?

I have been thinking so much abou props. Some questions have amassed: If th prop is the gun on stage but the play isn starting, isn't the gun still active? What's th line between a prop and a puppet? Whe does an artwork in art history become prop? When does its function becom subservient?

Greetings from the countryside, it i snowing . . . and today my friend's kid looke at me and said, "Hey, Rin, why are we mad of water instead of slime?"

Nina Beier: I just did this large-scal

nstallation in the countryside in Denmark vith grey-haired smokers blowing smoke ngs on twenty-two toppled lions, and now nat I have resurfaced I feel very ready and n shape to get going with developing this ew installation and hope we can get our ands on marble lions?

Cooper Jacoby: I found the conversation round the mis-localization of sound, iscrepancies between sound and visual ource, and how plastic/integrated the enses are really useful for the thermostat project I've been developing. One aspect want to explore in that project is how priming, priors, and semantic associations operate within the repeated exposure to n idiomatic phrase. I want to see if it is

During his wanderings across the Mediterranean, Odysseus has the sky above him and the sea below him for ten years. The Greeks on the beach who besieged Troy for ten years were aware of the sea behind them and the sky over them. "Here," Gladstone writes, "Homer had before him the most perfect example of blue. Yet he never once so describes the sky. His *ouranos* is starry, or broad, or great, or iron, or copper; but it is never blue . . . a child of three years in our nurseries knows, that is to say sees, more of colour than the man who founded . . . the sublime office of the poet."[8]

Later, others scrutinized ancient Icelandic, Hindu, Chinese, Arabic, and Hebrew writings and likewise found no mention of a word for blue. In fact, in most languages, the word for blue emerges as the last major color. The sole exception among the ancient civilizations is Egypt, where the color was produced artificially. Egyptian blue. Apparently, we perceive what we ourselves are able to make.

possible to encode familiarity at a sub- c semi-perceptual level.

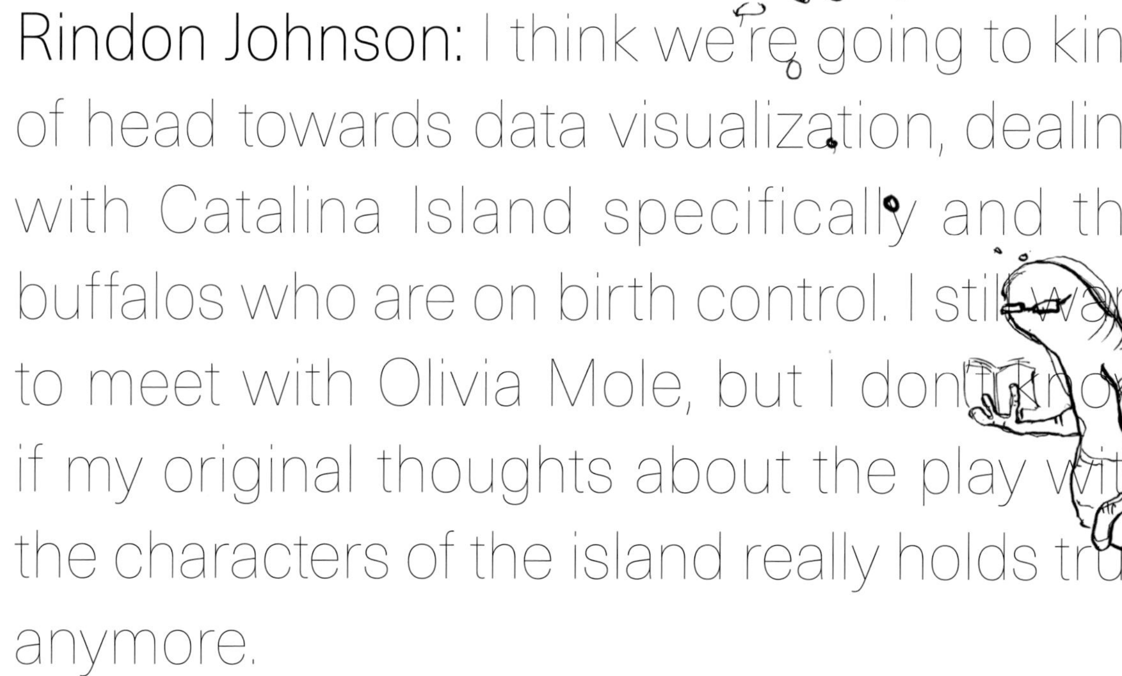

Rindon Johnson: I think we're going to kin of head towards data visualization, dealin with Catalina Island specifically and th buffalos who are on birth control. I still war to meet with Olivia Mole, but I don't know if my original thoughts about the play wit the characters of the island really holds tru anymore.

Aram Moshayedi: There is something deepl emotional to what you are circling, and I ar left wanting to have more of that emotiona investment as a reader of this text. Your use of language has such an ability to ensnar ne reader, and (I hope this doesn't sound oo wicked) I think you should try to use nis power a bit more to your advantage in nanipulating emotions. Manipulation is such dirty word, I hope you know what I mean.

There are moments when the text eels grounded in the place where it will ventually be performed. These moments nchor us to the place, it's a very light touch. ecurity Teaches a Lesson is the most *angible* scene in this regard. There is a irectness and immediacy to this passage nat is clear, the language of this passage s more inhabitable than the others. ~~That eing said, I don't want to push you too nuch into the direction of locating the text vithin the museum. It's great that it touches ipon this architectural and social context out it needn't be too overly present.~~

For hundreds of thousands of years, people roamed around as nomads. In their cave paintings, there were tones of red, black, brown, and ochre in all shades, but no blue, no green, and rarely white. When they became sedentary, they painted with red and yellow, but not with blue. Humans learned to imitate, produce, and master the color blue only late and with effort.

In South America, Asia, and Africa, where the indigo bush grows, fabrics have been dyed blue for at least six thousand years. The ancient Celtic and Germanic peoples also had a penchant for blue, which they fabricated from the woad plant. The ancient Greeks and Romans did know these plants, but they didn't have much use for them. The Romans in particular abhorred the color. They felt blue was barbaric and associated it with the body painting of intractable people at the margins of the empire, such as Germanic tribes and Scottish Picts. No wonder that in Latin the two words for blue arise late and come from elsewhere: the Germanic *blavus*, from which English *blue* and French *bleu* are derived, and the Arabic *azureus*. *Azureus* is descended from the Afghan-Persian word *lāzaward* and originally referred to the blue mineral stone lapis lazuli. The French *azur*, the Italian *azzurro*, the Polish *lazur*, Romanian *azur*, the Portuguese and Spanish *azul*, Hungarian *azúr*, and the Catalan *atzur*, all come from the name and color of lapis lazuli.

Asher Hartman: I do envision these a fragments that tear into space, in som cases, that happen unexpectedly and als perhaps happen formally. I am less intereste in devising a piece for a seated/structure audience than thinking about other ways c using space and time performatively.

These pieces will surely never happe one right after the other. I can imagine som lines being spoken days apart from othe lines, for example, that they are deprived c context.

Emotion is an interesting conundrur for me. I think what I'm interested in, i performance, is the push/pull between th expectation of catharsis, emotion, narrativ and the way we hint at, blunt, undercu emotion, how language deadens feelin as well. We use it to fill up space, to prov xistence.

I love the way people talk in life because anguage often reveals how disassociated ve can be from ourselves. Our unconscious naterial emerges in the banal, especially in he way speech is crafted to suggest but ot expose feeling.

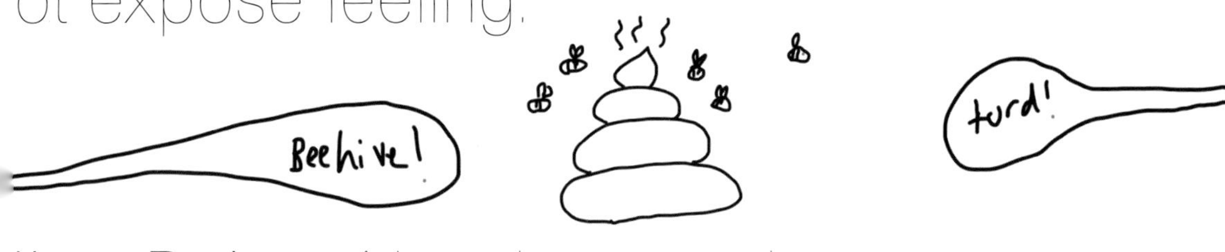

Jina Beier: Also, I wanted to suggest an rtist who could maybe interpret Asher's ext into a slow-riding performance on the ons. Their name is Bob Kil.

dania Shibli: I'm not sure this is the direction explore in relation to the text, which is bout "relations," or their non-existence, as an be traced between sound and image

Not until a thousand years later does the color blue make its solemn entrance in the West. In the Europe of the eleventh and twelfth centuries, stained-glass windows, dishes, fabrics, and clothing became blue. The legend of King Arthur associates him with the color, which gradually attains royal distinction. Blue becomes the color of the sky in painting, and—most importantly—Mary, the Mother of Christ, is depicted wearing a blue robe. From these origins, blue began its triumphal march in the West.[9]

If the patron's coffers permitted it, painters always chose the pigment ultramarine, which was considered the most beautiful, brilliant, and enduring blue. It was so precious that it was weighed with gold. Ultramarine is extracted from lapis lazuli. This iridescent blue stone is often embedded with the gold-colored particles of pyrite and has borne such diverse names as *azzurrum ultramarinum*, *azzurro oltramarino*, *azur d'Acre*, *pierre d'azur*, and *Lasurstein*.

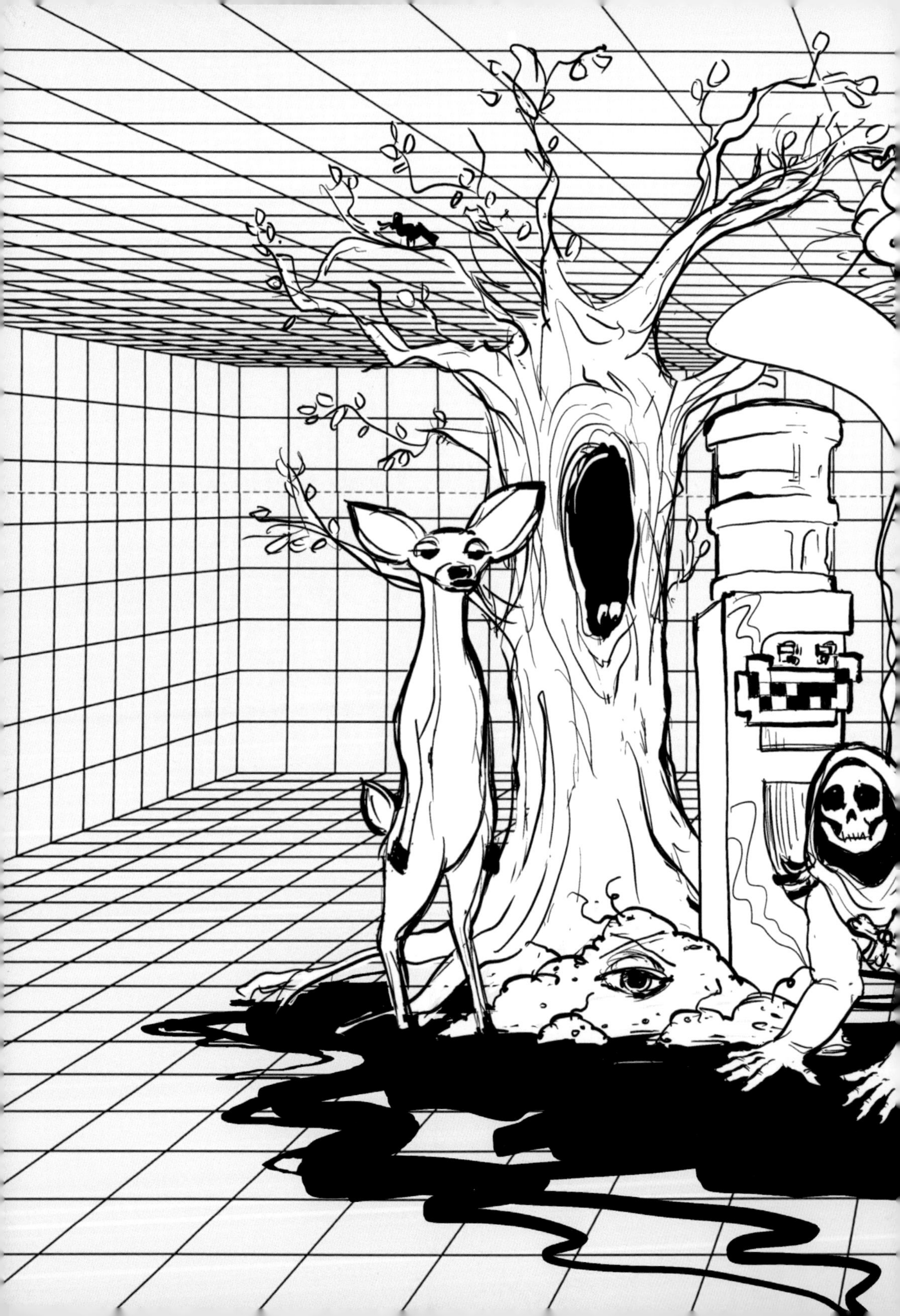

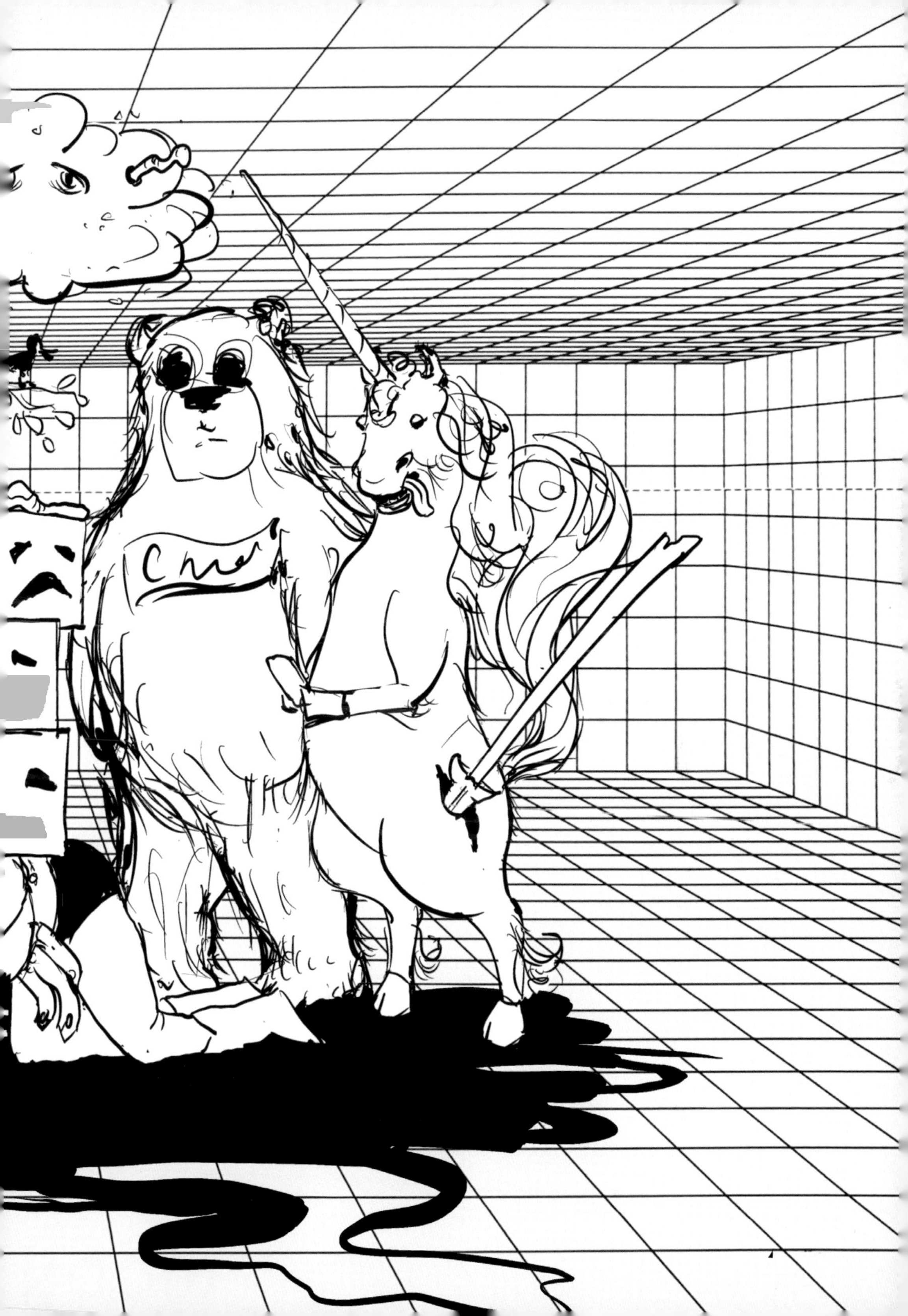

Highly sought after by Renaissance painters, ultramarine adorns Michelangelo's Sistine Chapel. It appears in *Girl with a Pearl Earring* (c. 1665), by the Dutch Golden Age painter Johannes Vermeer, whose weakness for the color is said to have driven his family to financial ruin. In the nineteenth century, French and Russian scientists finally succeeded in producing ultramarine synthetically, but this did no harm to its attractive power. Even today, the blue of the flag of the European Union is ultramarine. When the flag was presented in 1955, the Council of Europe officially explained the color by saying that it was "the blue sky of the Western world."[10] Five years later, the artist Yves Klein announced the "invention" of International Klein Blue (IKB), a customized variant of his favorite color, ultramarine. In 1993, Derek Jarman used a sole shot of IKB as the backdrop for the entirety of his experimental film *Blue*, his final creation.[11]

For centuries the material found in the most precious paintings in Western culture flowed forth from a few holes in a single Afghan mountain range, Sar-e-Sang, which means something like “the head of stone.” From here, lapis lazuli and the ultramarine derived from it found their way to Italy via the Silk Road.[12] The Venetian merchants who purchased it in Damascus or Cairo did not know exactly from whence it came.[13] Its origin was always mysterious; all that was known was that it was farther away than the east coast of the Mediterranean. This is why it was first called *transmarine* and later *ultramarine* (beyond the sea). Ultramarine is present-day Afghanistan.

despite their seeming interconnectednes

How different can an image in th practices of the colonizers be as oppose to the word/sound of that of the colonized This is what I feel can be an urgent matte to explore with the question on the relatio between both I've been posing and therefor brought to the context of your salade mix

Adam Linder: I feel the show needs to gra more wholeheartedly at what is the fram or the methodology that it wants to comm to . . . interdisciplinarity as assimilatior disciplinary fluidity, little nodes that grov an extra appendage kind of vibe. Mayb it's about looking at the whole ecology an how it's moving.

And so what we're saying is tha

ctually there's this space and a series of ncounters that can somewhat be related to ne another and a cosmology that's being reated, but they're not representing the ingularity. They're representing a collective orm of ideas that are all getting around omething. And again, it's like a postscript. Ve don't even know what the fuck it is, until 's like, kind of done.

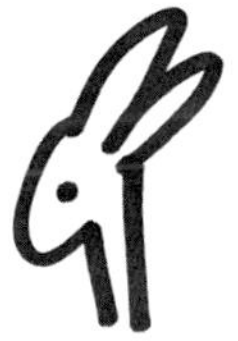

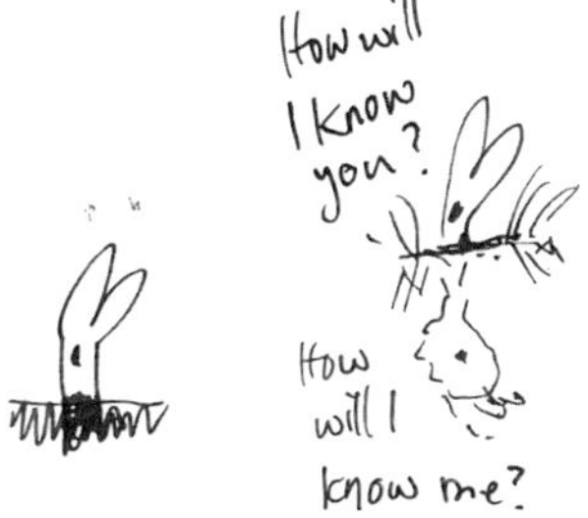

ahim Amir: Drawing on collective feminist ractices from the 1960s to the 1990s, the erm "project exhibition" has been coined or an artistic practice that transformed xhibition making "into a medium, into n intervention and a form of political rticulation" (Marion von Osten, 2010). Sonic Services employs this hybrid practice that

Lapis lazuli is considered the first "globally" traded commodity. The deep blue stones have traveled for six thousand years from the inaccessible province of Badakhshan in northeastern Afghanistan to Harappa, Egypt, Mesopotamia, Sumer, and Babylon. The death mask of the Egyptian pharaoh Tutankhamun has eyebrows made of lapis lazuli set in pure gold. The Bible often speaks of sapphires, but scholars agree that this refers to lapis lazuli.

Today, lapis lazuli is part of Afghanistan's mineral and gas resources, the value of which is estimated at a trillion US dollars. This wealth might be a curse. A Russian military officer once called a lapis lazuli mine a "general of war": "It will itself make people fight."[14] Even the Taliban have been unable to infiltrate the mountains of Badakhshan. Yet since the first war of the twenty-first century began, mismanagement and corruption have been impoverishing the population. They are forced to watch as the profits drain away, leaving them behind with empty stomachs and hands as well as ruined lungs and roads. About half of the profit from lapis lazuli now goes directly into the pockets of the Taliban. Today, lapis lazuli is popular as a power stone in the global esoteric scene, yet every blue stone purchased destabilizes the region and promotes the war in Afghanistan.

does not take the creation of a discrete an
finished artwork as the central objectiv
(while producing them as well along th
way), but emphasizes a) transformativ
and generative processes among thos
involved in the making of the exhibition; b
the shaping of discourses; c) the productio
of publics through a hybrid practice betwee
art, theory, research, curating, design, an
Institutional Critique that is characterized b
disciplinary flexibility; d) the questioning o
the relations of its own practice to broade
cultural and economic processes; an
e) an investment in the development o
subject figurations that can help navigat
nonhegemonic practices.

Asher Hartman: It really does feel like a

hese disciplines are talking to each other, ut in a kind of splintered way, splintered n a good way. How do you allow these xperiences to flow through one another n a way that eliminates hierarchy?

Like when you're walking in the forest, nd you see two tree branches that have allen across each other. Or a little brook hat you didn't know. That to me feels a ttle bit like the piece, in a good way. Like here's intersection, invention, surprise, rickle down, trickle out. Places where, you now, something that's visual is allowed to e and not necessarily messed with by the erformer. And somehow, this idea of the xhibition as something that consumes you.

I guess the word that keeps coming ack to me is *feral*.

To me, when I go into a museum, I feel

That sounds unromantic, especially in light of the fact that, since Novalis's tale *Heinrich von Ofterdingen* (1802), in which the hero dreams of a blue flower and sets off in search of it, blue has been considered the color of Romanticism, and the search for the blue flower has been a symbol of poetic desire. Things were also unromantic on the indigo plantations of Bengal, when brown people in the British colonial system were forced to produce the dye that colored textiles blue all over the world. Blue became the color of uniforms for the military, the police, and laborers (navy blue, blue line, blue collar), and later an anti-uniform emblem: for a long time, the blue in blue jeans was denim dyed with Indian blue. The plantation workers rebelled in the Blue Mutiny of the 1850s and 1860s.

Not much later, a color yet again excited colonial minds: Indian yellow. In the nineteenth century, this color had become popular with British and German painters for reproducing skin colors, especially darker shades. Artists had long painted Native American and Caribbean peoples with the same colors. Nude depictions were common, but the question of complexion remained contentious, imprecise, and unpredictable. While some regarded it as the worst failure of a painter if the observer could not tell what skin color a portrait subject had, others argued that every painter must decide individually whether to "exalt, diminish, or neutralize the dominant tint of a given complexion."[15] Indian yellow and its mixtures helped to develop a colonial color palette. Enthused by how brilliantly and precisely the most diverse skin tones could now be presented, art teachers in the 1860s began working out skin-color charts and standardizing color terminology, like "dusky" and "pale."

my own phlegm, my snot, my farts, excesse
of my body that aren't supposed to be ther
I imagine the people who work there do
have bodily fluids. That they are clean in
way I'm not. And so my body—my body-lik
body—is very apparent to me.

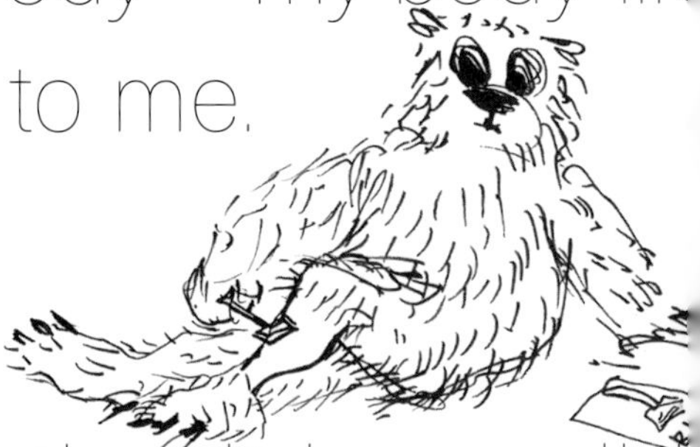

Nina Beier: So exciting that it is possib
to make Bob Kil the in-house artist for th
show. We will work on this in the next day
and get back with more concrete though
after we speak with Asher Hartman, bu
for now I will send some more links an
sketches and things for the lion search.

Bob Kil: I am digesting the idea of being a
in-house artist, wow. I think the performanc

an grow, shape-shift organically over the hree months. I will push the format with pen arms.

indon Johnson: Aram Moshayedi brought p the possibility of finding a department ı one of the universities around that might ave already done some work on Catalina hat we can build from. Aram and I also poke a little bit about purposeful inclusion e: L. Frank, wondering about how to best se museum resources for their benefit nd how we'd best go about incorporating heir work into our contribution given their nultivalent practice.

Cooper Jacoby: I feel the benches have

Thus the uproar was all the greater when, not long afterward, it came to light that the entire supply of Indian yellow in Bengal was manufactured from cows' urine and required forcing the cows to eat nothing but mangos and mango leaves. This made the cows sick, and very few of them survived the color diet longer than two years. The British government panicked, fearing that diet might develop into riot. This worry was justified, because the emerging animal protection movement was gaining attention at home, while in India a national movement had arisen that sanctified the cow and declared it the Mother of India. Colors had already become a catalyst of anti-colonial resistance in this region during the Blue Mutiny. A Yellow Revolution was to be avoided at all costs. The British government stepped in to hamper production of and trade in Indian yellow, because the aesthetic power of the color had come into conflict with its material production: "In short, the longstanding practice of depicting Indians on canvas had come into open conflict with the desire to govern them. By the 1920s, British artists were no longer painting flesh in the same range of colors."[16]

When, at the same time in the United States, photography and film were beginning to replace painting, the bodies of cows played a similarly central role. The term *film* derives from the gelatin film that was a medium for light-sensitive bromide. The Eastman Kodak Company, later a world leader in the production of photographic and film materials, was on the brink of ruin because a large number of their films exhibited irregular qualities, which led to spoiled photographs. The cause was traced to the gelatin extracted from slaughterhouse waste. Further studies showed that cows that had eaten mustard provided better photographic gelatin, because the sulfuric components in mustard oil accentuated the light sensitivity of the emulsion. Consequently, Kodak began strictly monitoring the cows' nutritional protocol. Modern black-and-white film was born in the bodies of cows, as the head of Kodak's research laboratory later reported: "Twenty years ago we found out that if cows didn't like mustard there wouldn't be any movies at all."[17]

both a functional role (gathering heat fc
the thermostats) and could play an auxiliar
role in the exhibition design—for viewin
or bracketing other works, overlapping wit
performance, etc. Perhaps their thermal
reactive surfaces can be an ambier
element that could recede and emerge i
a choreographed way.

Fahim Amir: I actually tried not to think abou
how to make an artwork out of my writte
contribution, but I tried to fuse armature
handles where people could grab onto
certain sentence, and then move their ow
thing around it.

Elke Auer: I imagine the structure made ou

f iron, painted black, and the ramp, platforms, nd colored elements made out of painted lywood, with a nod to the space-force-onstruction paintings of Lyubov Popova. he ramp will have no railing, as I was told hat animals who will be willing to go up here (cats/chicken/squirrels/chameleons) o not need railings. The base references ziggurat, an ancient structure associated vith the Tower of Babel, and the middle art with a visible iron structure will look lot like the simplified model of Vladimir atlin's *Monument to the Third International* hat was used for parades on the street. Vhereas the tip should look like termite rchitecture or a giant claw.

For me it is important to create a real ossibility for animals to use the ramps nd walk on the tower and not degrade

Colors are not simply there, they are made. And their aesthetics have a history.[18] Only relatively recently did the standardized, industrial producibility of colors discipline their unruliness.[19] Before that, colors had an aura of mystery. Often, their production was secret, their effects unclear, and their origin “elsewhere.” Perhaps that is why Western philosophy has mistrusted colors so much that it can rightly be accused of chromophobia.[20]

Today, more and more voices are demanding a decolonization of thinking—a reconceptualization of the West and its logics as privileged sites of history. It is time to augment this movement with a *decolonization of the senses*. This includes ideas of the aesthetic order that reach deep into science. When Isaac Newton demystified the colors of light by directing light through a prism and breaking it up into its component colors, it took him years to decide how many colors there actually were. Newton was convinced of the analogy between audible tones and visible colors. Hence, from the spectrum of visible light, he chose, in accordance with the seven notes of the Doric scale, exactly seven colors: violet, indigo, blue, green, yellow, orange, and red. A different scientist with different aesthetic associations might have come to a different conclusion.

it to a gesture. We want this tower to b
a monument, a model, and a real useabl
architecture for smaller animals. I understan
that it might be difficult to get service animal
to use it, but I am all for coming up wit
ideas about how to do that or think abou
alternatives, like animal actors.

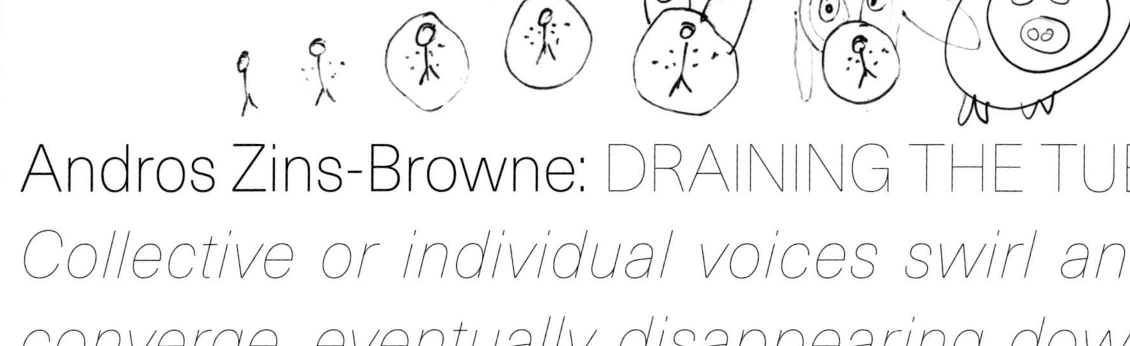

Andros Zins-Browne: DRAINING THE TUE
Collective or individual voices swirl an
converge, eventually disappearing dow
the drain into silence.

Jessika Kenney: What is it to have an ope
heart, or to have a functioning heart, to hav
that be audible in a voice? Maybe *functionin*
is actually a good word because it make

more dynamic instead of, like, you suffer, nd then you earn some new possession or roperty because you suffered (or someone lse suffered). It's like the functioning of a eart is audible, but the only way the heart an function is to perceive pain, to have the wareness of that feeling without shutting own. The voice has an activity that a heart oes. (A heart is listening and perceiving vhile inner and/or outer voices are doing hings.)

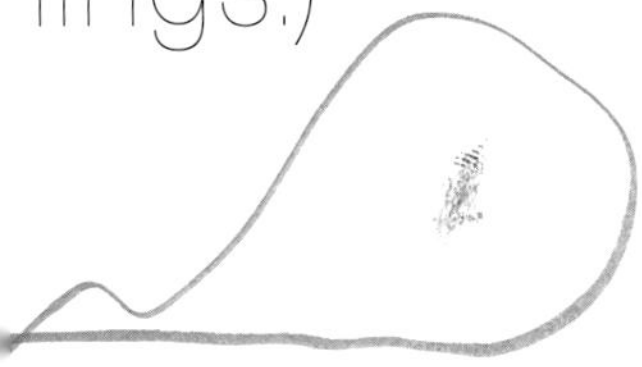

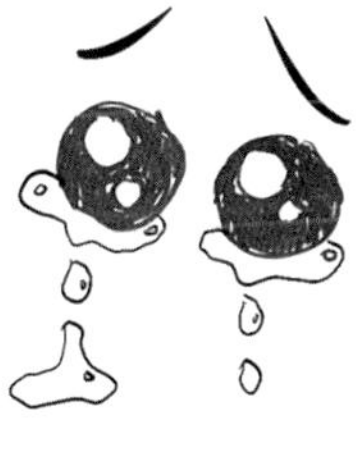

Adania Shibli: My concern is always how o allow words to have the freedom to be engaged with in as many ways as possible. Vould a possible collaboration pin the elation in question to one thing? The colonial element I referred to is one that might be

Seeing colors is considered a distant sense. But perhaps this is not the whole truth; it's possible that color perception is also a proximal sense—a sense of touch. Schwarte points out that the Greek word *chroma* "means color, but also skin color, complexion, and makeup. It is related to the word *chors*, which denotes skin, body, skin color, and also closest proximity." Color and body, *chroma* and *chors*, "are based on the verb *chrozein*: to touch, to coat, to color." Schwarte pleads for a "thinking in color" that grasps the world "through processes of touching and coloring" and "that breaks away from distancing cognitive encirclement, in favor of a process of touch that makes sure of presence, consistency, and physicality."[21]

This is not a mere marginal note. Which terms, stories, and images we use to describe our forms of thinking and our modes of perception influence both of these. If colors have bodies, their perception is also a touching of our own bodies. Thinking in color would mean withstanding this and allowing ourselves to be touched. “There is nothing that man fears more than the touch of the unknown,” Elias Canetti writes as the opening sentence of his seminal treatise *Crowds and Power*.[22] He also says he thinks in animals the way others think in concepts.[23] Perhaps this would be a further aspect of thinking in color.

behind the source of these questions, but n
the only one, so how to keep that possibilit
actually and really there? ~~The proposal t~~
~~bring the UCLA Multisensory Processin~~
~~Lab to experiment with a political situation~~
~~also in that questionable duality; the seen an~~
~~said/heard, the scientific and nonscientifi~~
~~the objective and subjective. Their sterilit~~
~~of perception and description is one that i~~
~~certainly political, though a denied one, so~~
~~can be inspiring for a political question to b~~
~~brought to a lab situation, with all that the la~~
~~can offer. Aren't you bringing words to th~~
~~exhibition space? These are my question~~
~~back.~~

Ralph Lemon: Rant, as you may hav
gathered, is its own beast, and has

eculiar agency. It can demand a lot from its
nomentary landings. And then it disappears.

ndros Zins-Browne: DOODLING: *Vocally oodling. An idea, meandering, not articularly committed to destination or ying to achieve a particular form, thinking ut loud in thought, tryin' shit 'n' tryin' shit, racticing possible propositions. A mode of ehearsal and sketch.*

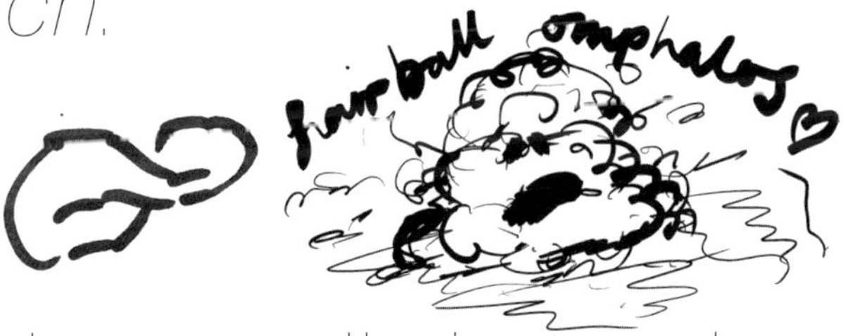

ram Moshayedi: I am really just trying to nderstand how and why performance r liveness exists in a museum without ecoming an instrument or tool or absorbed nto museology or consumed by an xhibitionary logic.

Color is so much a part of life that even the occurrence of death manifests itself in colors. The fourth stage of death and one of its most visible signs is *livor mortis*, the name ancient Romans and modern medicine give to the bluishness of death. “So it’s true: Being without Being is blue,” the author William H. Gass wrote.[24] However, *livor* denotes not only bluishness and bruising in general but also a black or blue mark. Just as English has *black eye* and German has *blaues Auge* (blue eye), the body is the locus where colors are uncertain to this day.

Out of the blue is associated with suddenness, unexpectedness, and groundlessness, perhaps because for many people the divine dwells in the blue heavens above. Absolute, divine power is unlimited, not subject to any other will or law. It can strike you without warning, like a stroke of lightning "out of a clear blue sky." Not long ago, a young boy from the border area between Afghanistan and Pakistan explained in a congressional briefing how something that isn't owned can still be stolen: "I no longer love blue skies. In fact, I now prefer grey skies. The drones do not fly when the skies are grey."[25]

Elke Auer: When I first read your descriptio
of the exhibition, I had the feeling there
a little bit of romanticizing theater work—
romantic idea of how theater works. Fro
what I have experienced, theater is a ver
hierarchized environment in which th
narrative of the genius director is still ver
much alive. So my first question to yo
would be, are you more interested in th
process, like in the collaborative knowledg
production, or in the outcome? I'm usuall
more interested in the part that happen
on the so-called rehearsal stage wher
there's nothing fixed yet. The stage desig
is sketched out with spatial markers mad
out of cheap materials, and it feels more lik
a laboratory, a space to experiment. All th
potential is still there.

ram Moshayedi: How do performance nd liveness and the body retain solidity in n environment that absorbs it into its own nethodological program?

Because each work or contribution n the exhibition will have to be read in elationship to the others, trust has to be stablished. Some contributions will be nore ambient, scenographic, ever-present, vhile others may be more episodic and eeting. But cohabitation within the overall nvironment becomes part of the puzzle ve're working to solve in a way that serves ne interests of each individual contributor. 'he hope is that the result produces omething where authorship is retained hough there is also something more of a omposition being formed or something nore akin to a living assemblage.

In German, *ins Blaue hinein* (into the blue) means doing something indefinite, tenuous, and uncertain. *Into the blue* means looking into the vast, the immeasurable, the nebulous. In 1797, the policeman of philosophy, Immanuel Kant, warned in his essay *Proclamation of the Imminent Conclusion of a Treaty of Perpetual Peace in Philosophy*: "A critical philosophy is one . . . that does not just philosophize into the blue."[26]

Perhaps we need more thinking into the blue these days. It may be that philosophers are less well equipped for this than poets or thinkers who are both, like Ernst Bloch. Bloch's *The Principle of Hope* begins with a section titled *Daily into the Blue*. Here the poet of light writes: "The child wants to be a bus-conductor or a confectioner. Seeks long journeys, far away, cake every day. That seems like real living. With animals too we dream we are big. With small ones especially, they are less frightening, they run into our hands. Or can be caught in nets; distant wishing becomes active in this way."[27] For him, color is the abyss and the horizon of the present.

Morag Keil: The move to a community cente
model for museums has really stuck with m
but the very nature of museums being kind
anti-human, as in anti-touch, and oxyge
and fingerprints sweat and secretions fror
humans being the things the museums try t
protect the works from. so i wanted this to b
featured in the work. ~~for now i'm thinking t~~
~~have puke over things like sealed w varnis~~
~~but something super directly gross and flui~~
~~and corrosive.~~ its quite cartoony in my hea
atm, but maybe also have a bit of the roug
aesthetic. puke is good cause it's the inside
coming out. i was listening to this full thin
about relationship to the other about wha
we put in our bodies or how close we ar
to others physically and mentally and als
sort of relating to skin disorders as its th
thing between the inside and the outsid

ut like the kinda psychological element f skin disorders but yeah puke is like a hysical thing that crosses outside to inside nd back again.

i had this idea a while ago to make these ıbes from this reality show here in the uk alled *supersize vs superskinny*. its a show where they get people with disordered ating to swap diets for a week or something nd live in this house together, its very mean eality tv like contemporary freak show, they ut ppls weekly intake into a tube to shame nem. but i never made it cause felt too veird about it coming from this show but i ked the idea of these tubes filed with layers f something, i mean it could be printed so s not actual food. but the kinda contained ness and the way its like mimicking the ody in size-ish and that u fill it.

Bloch was writing *The Principle of Hope* during the bleakness of the Second World War. But color as a prerequisite for the creation of new forms of life is something we already encounter in his earliest reflections. In 1918, the mass death of the First World War is past, Red October sends its reverberations out into the world, and the young philosopher publishes his first book, *The Spirit of Utopia*. Its foreword closes with these words: “Only in us does this light still burn, and we are beginning a fantastic journey toward it, a journey toward the interpretation of our waking dream, toward the implementation of the central concept of utopia. To find it, to find the right thing, for which it is worthy to live, to be organized, and to have time: that is why we go, why we cut new, metaphysically constitutive paths, summon what is not, build into the blue, and build ourselves into the blue, and there seek the true, the real, where the merely factual disappears—*incipit vita nova*.”[28] New life begins.

Notes

1. Julia Kristeva, *Desire in Language: A Semiotic Approach to Literature and Art* (New York: Columbia University Press, 1980), 221.
2. Vilém Flusser, "Farben statt Formen," *Lob der Oberflächlichkeit. Für eine Phänomenologie der Medien* (Mannheim, Germany: Bollmann, 1993), 123.
3. Ludger Schwarte, *Denken in Farbe. Zur Epistemologie des Malens* (Berlin: August Verlag, 2020), 137.
4. See Schwarte, *Denken in Farbe*, 117–41.
5. D. Dipon Ghosh et al., "C. Elegans Discriminates Colors to Guide Foraging," *Science* 371, no. 6533 (2021), 1059–63.
6. R. Drew Griffith, "Gods' Blue Hair in Homer and in Eighteenth-Dynasty Egypt," *The Classical Quarterly*, New Series 55, no. 2 (2005), Cambridge University Press, 329–34. See also Anne Carson, "Variations on the Right to Remain Silent," *A Public Sphere*, no. 7 (2008).
7. R. Rutherfurd-Dyer, "Homer's Wine-Dark Sea," *Greece & Rome* 30, no. 2 (1983), Cambridge University Press, 125–28.
8. William E. Gladstone, *Studies on Homer and the Homeric Age*, vol. 3 (Oxford, England: Oxford University Press, 1858), 483. See also Carson, "Variations on the Right to Remain Silent."
9. See Michel Pastoureau, *Blue: The History of a Color* (Princeton, NJ: Princeton University Press, 2001).
10. "Flag of Europe," Wikipedia, https://en.wikipedia.org/wiki/Flag_of_Europe.
11. Andrew Wilson, "Derek Jarman: *Blue*, 1993" (2013), Tate, https://www.tate.org.uk/art/artworks/jarman-blue-t14555.
12. Jean Wyart, Pierre Bariand, and Jean Filippi, "Lapis-Lazuli from Sar-E-Sang, Badakhshan, Afghanistan," *Gems & Gemology* 17, no. 4 (Winter 1981), 184–90.
13. Andrea Mozzato, "The Pigment Trade in Venice and the Mediterranean in the Second Half of the Fifteenth Century," in *Renaissance Studies in Honor of Joseph Connors*, ed. Machtelt Israëls and Louis A. Waldman, Villa I Tatti Series 29 (Cambridge, MA: Harvard University Press, 2013), 171–79; William Eamon, "Pharmaceutical Self-Fashioning or How to Get Rich and Famous in the Renaissance Medical Marketplace," *Pharmacy in History* 45, no. 3 (2003), 123–29.
14. "War in the Treasury of the People: Afghanistan, Lapis Lazuli and the Battle for Mineral Wealth," Global Witness report 83, no. 3 (June 2016), https://www.globalwitness.org/documents/18528/war_in_the_treasury_printv6a_lr_G2pfYBL.pdf.
15. Jordanna Bailkin, "Indian Yellow: Making and Breaking the Imperial Palette," *Journal of Material Culture* 10, no. 2 (2005), 201.
16. Bailkin, "Indian Yellow," 208.
17. Dr. C.E. Kenneth Mees, quoted in Nicole Shukin, *Animal Capital: Rendering Life in Biopolitical Times* (Minneapolis: University of Minnesota Press, 2009), 109.
18. See Natasha Eaton, *Colour, Art and Empire: Visual Culture and the Nomadism of Representation* (London: I.B. Tauris, 2013); Michael Taussig, *What Color Is the Sacred?* (Chicago: University of Chicago Press, 2011); and Regina Lee Blaszczyk, "Chromophilia: The Design World's Passion for Colour," *Journal of Design History* 27, no. 3 (2014), 203–17.
19. Regina Lee Blaszczyk and Uwe Spiekermann, eds., *Bright Modernity: Color, Commerce, and Consumer Culture* (New York: Palgrave Macmillan, 2017).
20. See David Batchelor, *Chromophobia* (London: Reaktion, 2013).
21. Schwarte, *Denken in Farbe*, 29.
22. Elias Canetti, *Crowds and Power* (New York: Continuum Publishing, 1962), 15.
23. See Elias Canetti, *Über Tiere*, ed. Brigitte Kronauer (Frankfurt, Germany: Fischer, 2017).
24. William H. Gass, *On Being Blue: A Philosophical Inquiry* (New York: New York Review Books, 1991), 12. See also Maggie Nelson, *Bluets* (Seattle: Wave Books, 2009).
25. Alexander Abad-Santos, "This 13-Year-Old Is Scared When the Sky Is Blue Because of Our Drones," *The Atlantic*, October 29, 2013, https://www.theatlantic.com/politics/archive/2013/10/saddest-words-congresss-briefing-drone-strikes/354548/.
26. Immanuel Kant, *Kant's gesammelte Schriften*. Die königlich preussische Akademie der Wissenschaften, vol. VIII (Berlin: G. Reimer, 1900), 416. This is the author's translation, since the original German passage "*nicht so ins Blaue hinein vernünftelt*" was translated rather loosely as "that does not engage in vacuous hair-splitting" by Peter Heaths, in Henry Allison, Peter Heath, and Immanuel Kant, *Theoretical Philosophy After 1781 (The Cambridge Edition of the Works of Immanuel Kant in Translation)* (Cambridge, England: Cambridge University Press, 2002), 455.
27. Ernst Bloch, *The Principle of Hope*, vol. 1, Studies in Contemporary German Social Thought (Cambridge, MA: MIT Press, 1995), 21.
28. Ernst Bloch, *The Spirit of Utopia* (Stanford, CA: Stanford University Press, 2000), 3.

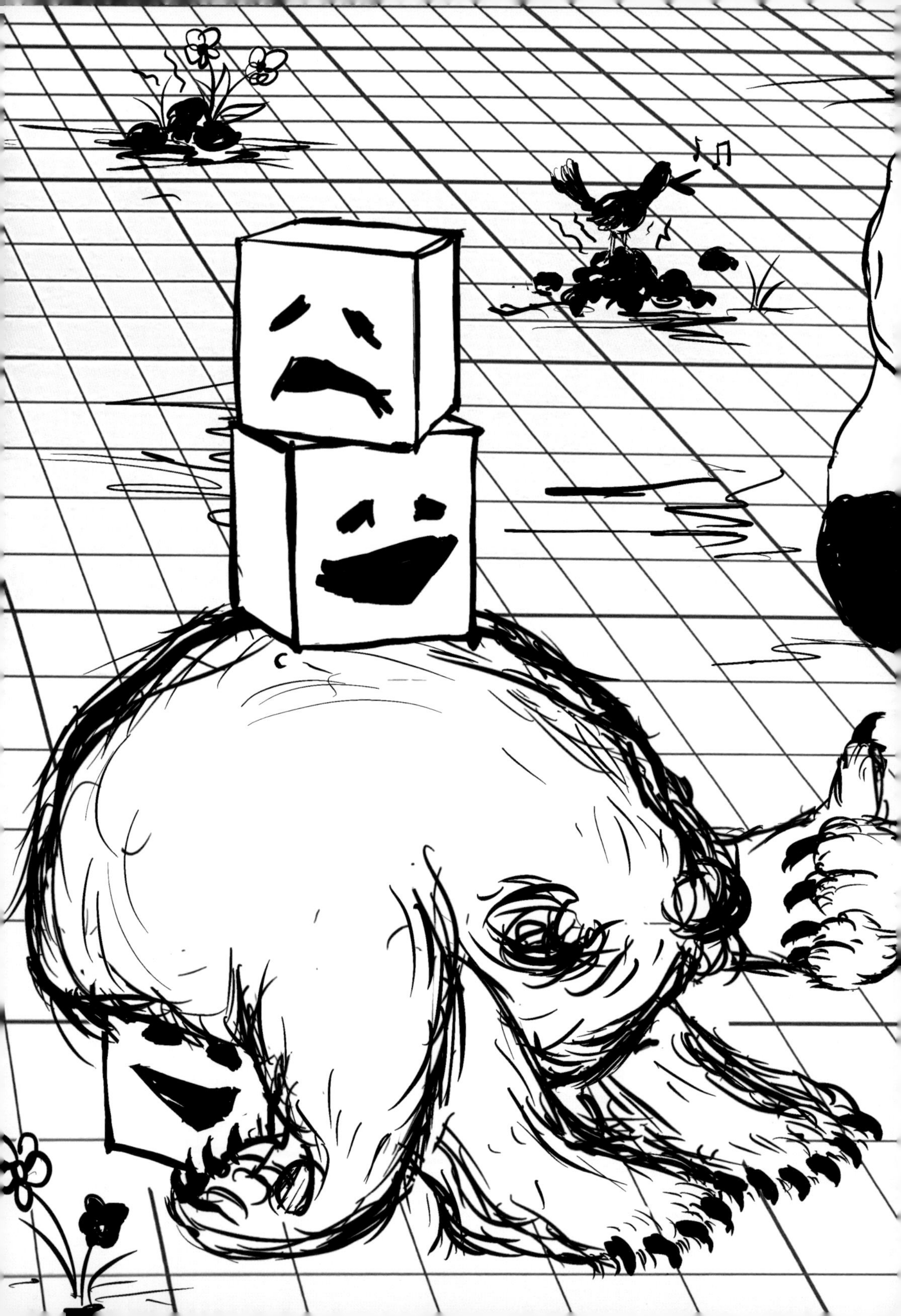

Animal Regret: Five Dances

ASHER HARTMAN

These scripts are meant to be embodied, to be said aloud, to be inflected by gesture. They are broken apart, never delivered one after the other, always scattered throughout the institution. They happen upon the visitor, in bursts, in corners, in curated rooms. No stages. They are not plays but rather indications of a dance. If you're gonna read them, stick out your tongue, jut your hip, growl, allow for insinuating pauses, rock your head. They are full of air to accommodate the performer's gestures, looks, pouts, taunts. The movers that play them should be savvy interlocutors between two worlds, the In and the Out, mounted by spirits or spirits themselves. The players should be the haughtiest of jokers; the richest of kleptomaniacs; furious survivors of triple-decker parking lots, keys in knuckles, moving too fast—people who know how to do it till it's done. Linguistic gestures are awkward snakes and body rolls, shaking fields of cellulite in fabulously wide asses, ripped jeans, nose grease, and hair that can't be controlled.

Jules Gimbrone: I think I am getting
handle on the type of work I would like t
propose for the show. I think that it woul
be nice to develop sculptural apparatuse
that would lead to perceptual dissonance c
dissociation by the viewer/listener. I woul
like to exploit the vulnerabilities of sensor
manipulation, specifically sight and sounc
that we discussed with Dr. Ladan Sham
and potentially work with her in developin
the content for these systems. I have som
ideas for forms and shapes that would b
interesting sculpturally and conceptually i
conceiving these states of dissociation, an
I think the size and number of them woul
be contingent on the budget.

Micah Silver and I met and we discusse
the idea of collaborating on a mechanism t
capture Schlieren images in real time. Thi

deo/photographic set-up would function oth as a type of "stage" and sculpture rough which to capture air flow and novement, energy transfer, and/or sound vaves and make them visible.

indon Johnson: Kite and I are keeping urselves very open as we collect data nd research during our visit. Our practices ntersect at many points, but I might eneralize that we find common footing n our uses of technology, mapping, data, nd form. We are hoping to learn more bout how our nonhuman counterparts on ne island are living alongside us human ctors, how we are affecting each other, ow that can be measured, and about how nat relationship has changed over time.

CAST

(All can be played by one person)

OBVIOUSLY FEMALE she's like she cares and she doesn't care

CHARACTER malleable, up for anything, can change on a dime

COMEDIAN a bear, tolerant, allergies, old-school Jewish, or fake

PORN STAR nice boy, built, groomed, late twenties

TYRA, PLEASE STEP FORWARD: INTRODUCTION TO A DANCE

Starring
OBVIOUSLY FEMALE

It is OBVIOUSLY FEMALE, worn out from the sex trade of right foot, left foot, who can still dance. I, whose hair has been permed one too many times, whose raccoon eyes flash above a Mars bar crammed into a pink pucker. I, whose stink fogs the institutional mirrors. It is I who runs the show. I pounce on a gig like this.

We see a gallery, a palace of cheap fluorescent rectangles, colored, fabulous. We see four actors, automatons, systems, fakes, illuminated, quiescent, serious, stately. Perhaps one holds a walkie-talkie, possible '80s spy. All are dressed in relative comfort without sacrificing fashion. Contemporary. American, no-nonsense. In contrast, OBVIOUSLY FEMALE wears spaghetti straps, rhinestones, a whirling poly circle skirt. How does this female know so much in her own body? She gestures, moves, flows. Her speech is lilting, following her gestures, broad sweeps.

Recently we welcomed artist and Tongv
elder L. Frank into our collaborative circl
and our hope is to return to the island wit
L. Frank to learn more about Pimu and th
island's deep significance. We have foun
ourselves running the gamut of materi
interests for this project and the more w
learn about the island, the more shape ou
project will take. I hope this summation isn
too general as we are still finding our wa
through the many intersections that interes
us about Pimu. So far we have planned t
see the island through the colonizer's len
and to learn as much as we can about a
the woven threads that make up its curren
state. We're really looking forward to learnin
more about the island and the Wrigle
Institute for Environmental Studies.

sher Hartman: Here are some descriptors:

CHARACTER

Male, very good shape-shifter.

As SECURITY, thick, beefy, sweaty, nervous, Brooklyn born; nice guy; father, trying to do the best he can. Doesn't want to scare or hurt people. Been around the block many times; military, security, department store cop, late shifts okay. Agile, acrobat a plus. A true angel.

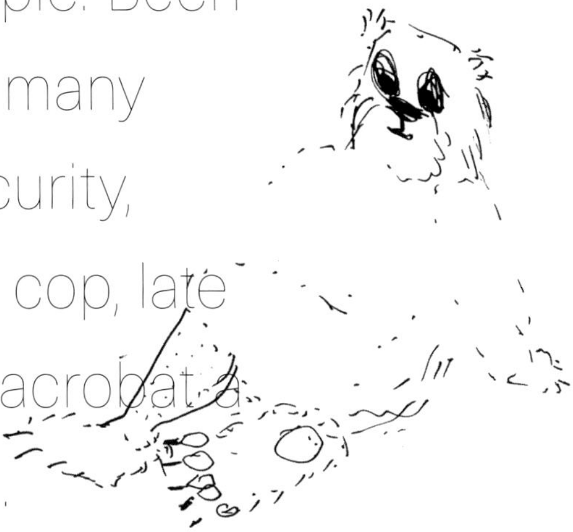

OBVIOUSLY FEMALE May I circle my foot? May I carve out a hexagon? May I . . . uh? Dip and . . . flex and . . . posture? May I speak with a tongue with a blade in it? May I . . . ? Uh. Dig you. Uh.

You approach. She sees you. She brings her hands to her clavicle, tilts her head, postures, leans back.

OBVIOUSLY FEMALE Oh, who? As if you didn't know. Let me introduce you to my spirit guide, Gascon Rives. Gascon is a French bulldog, none other than. He makes me get down on my knees.

A small animatronic bulldog, Gascon Rives, trundles to her side.

OBVIOUSLY FEMALE Outta these walls walk Titans: Keanu Reeves (no relation), Tyra, Rosie Perez as Angel, and Special Guest, whose name cannot be revealed. It is through their electronic mastery that we have Art.

She moves, careens, bucks forward, backs away.

OBVIOUSLY FEMALE May I index with my big toe the scale of the universe? The cosmos? Time?

She confronts you in the nicest way.

OBVIOUSLY FEMALE I asked my spirit guide if I was gonna be famous, and he point-blank said, No.

She teases your friend.

OBVIOUSLY FEMALE I asked my spirit guide if anything was gonna come of this meeting of ours, and he point-blank said, No.

She introduces whimsy, a teacher.

OBVIOUSLY FEMALE The nautilus, the seashell, the golden rule, the Peruvian shamanic electric blue hover above us now like a craft. Thee Craft. Watch those tilted letters. They shine.

Wow! She is swept away by her own wonder, the strictness of her desire.

OBVIOUSLY FEMALE Shafts of light. There are shafts of light hitting us now. Shafts from the gaps in a Mad Max grin, broad shafts, hallelujah shafts, alien shafts, papal shafts, short shorts shafts, high-tops shafts, belly shafts, teachers 'n' preachers, and you know what, I really don't care.

She introduces the obvious.

In SKELETON PARTY, sad,
tired, has given up, nice
though, not making too
much of a fuss, arms by
the side, supine.

In M/OM, male, 40s plus,
tolerant, irritated, resigned,
carries mother's purse
but hates it; drives M/OM,
smart enough, eats silently;
large sandwiches, extra
pastrami, GPS in the car;
turns the radio up when
others are speaking, subtly,
old tunes, '30s and '40s
crooners preferred.

OBVIOUSLY FEMALE

The clear star, ex-coke fiend, good body for her age, great dancer, hair is fried from drugs and harsh chemicals, wears rhinestones in the day, maybe a sweater with a poly circle strappy skirt, lots of skin. Doesn't take shit. Will stab a finger in your clavicle if need be. Argues about prices. Talks aloud to self, mumbles. Laughs at her own jokes. Charges for her time. Not liking the museum space unless there are freebies, a handout would be

OBVIOUSLY FEMALE Can I lean over and say, I don't give a hoot about the thirteenth century? Now how about you?

She darts. She fingers the air.

OBVIOUSLY FEMALE What I want is a conception, something like a dripping clock. What I want is a checkerboard dream portal to open me up, to make me feel what it's all about.

She stops, clicks her tongue, tilts her head. A new beat. Fuck all that noise. The time is now. She takes us in a new direction, a little more '00s.

OBVIOUSLY FEMALE Say.

Pick it up. Pick it up. Head switches, cat's paws.

OBVIOUSLY FEMALE I was walking along when this boutique caught my eye. I was walking along, gonna cash my mother's checks, and then I saw it, this glowing cash register. I said to myself, let me dip in. And lo, what I saw freaked me out. I said, Trip on this. Trip on this. Say. In the future:

In the future, there will be spray-on experiences.

In the future, barbecue sauce will quell the amygdala's choking throttle.

In the future, you will program your mate from a sore in your DNA.

In the future, you will be able to say, with Certainty and Equanimity, that chick has no brains. Whooo!

All of these stars have their special gifts. Keanu, step forward.

The automaton steps forward, tall, stately, eyeline to the opposite wall.

OBVIOUSLY FEMALE Tyra, step forward.

Her eyes beaming, automaton Tyra obliges.

OBVIOUSLY FEMALE Rosie, please.

Very state capitol, Rosie automaton proceeds.

OBVIOUSLY FEMALE Special Guest, Gascon Rives—

Gascon performs a circlet. Wow!

OBVIOUSLY FEMALE These are my playthings.
These are my gods.

OBVIOUSLY FEMALE sweeps into position.

nice, a lollipop, a button, something. Wild-eyed. Furious. Indignant. Not going to be used, but in the end, sympathetic to others' pain. Indifferent to old men, unless there's something in it for her. Reasonable when approached with fairness. Funny. Resilient. Needs love, but not willing to be.

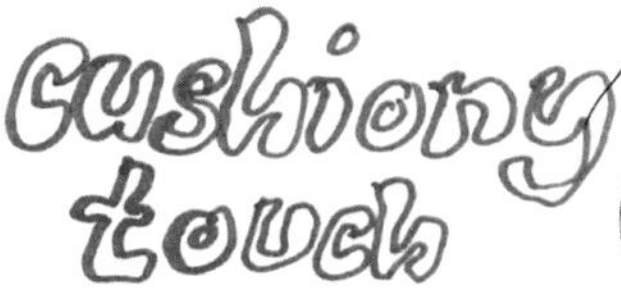

cushiony touch

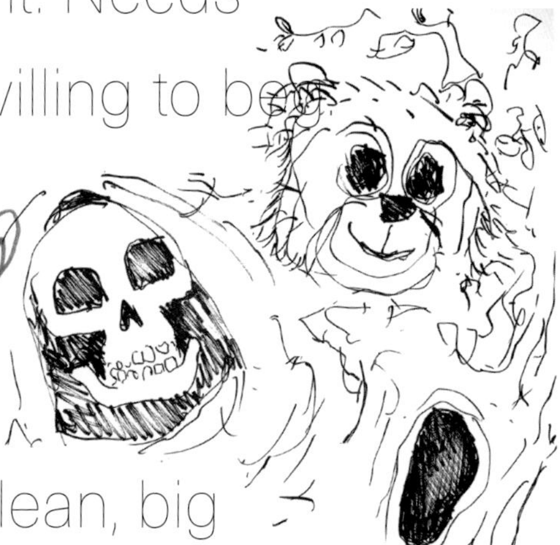

PORN STAR

Nice guy, cut, lean, big beefy, *masc.*, smart but not showy. Gym rat but keeps to himself. Professional, up and coming. Horticulturist.

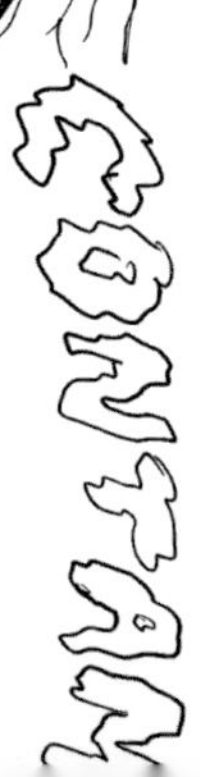

Interested in art and culture for the Insta, but you know, Paris is cool. Kind, really. Generous to his co-stars. This whole museum thing is a trip. Watch the older guys. Creepy, but okay. He is used to being asked dumb questions. Sex is health, friendly, good times.

COMEDIAN

Old, allergies, perpetually stuffed nose, suited, tired. Jewish, as in JEWISH!!!, gently inspired by Jackie Mason. Puts up with everything. Likes nothing.

OBVIOUSLY FEMALE First, Keanu, let me know that there is a raison d'être.

OBVIOUSLY FEMALE doesn't know what the fuck just happened.

OBVIOUSLY FEMALE Whoo!! Can you feel it?

Ty, let me know that there is recourse in "I don't know what the fuck just happened."

Rosie, let me take revenge with a needle in my arm that says, Charm wins out.

This is where the Special Guest and I do it, do it, do it, like it's never been done before.

Movement now, a twisting, sexy, vivifying dance, and—exeunt!

SKELETON PARTY

Starring
Character

CHARACTER

I lie in my bed as long as possible these days. Doin' well! I say to my neighbor, who passes by my open door. The thing they used to call my body will not sleep. The thing they called my mind concocts. In this dance I am CHARACTER, an unsexed non-mover whose impulses are colonic. This is a sickroom mystery. Death is as seen in pictures. I leave it to the choreographer to place us.

A steel guitar plays.

CHARACTER

Andy, I said, one morning, hearing some noise in the kitchen. Andy? But it was not Andy.

Death always comes to me as an intelligent man.

You never know what's inside, Death said, rifling through my cabinets looking for sugar for his tea. He wore a top hat, as he often does.

Yes, that's true, I said, out of guilt and shame.

A bear as in daddy bear,
like a bear, not an otter.
Thick, hairy, wheezing
occasionally. Life is as it is.
Does like the Oldsmobile
for some reason. Maybe a
bit of nostalgia.

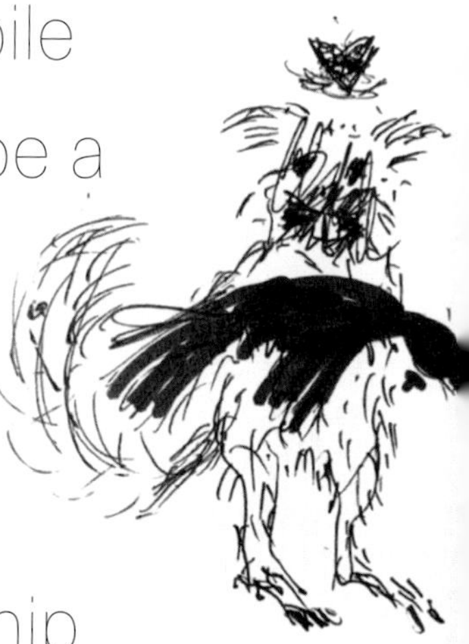

As M/OM, controlling, hip
to the mind games, self-
absorbed, lover of rich
and powerful men, short,
overly made up, red hair
dye is too much, no one
is fooled by the red hair.
Always searching in purse
for something, a Kleenex,
mostly. Lightly inspired by

Estelle Harris. Steely eyed.
Shifty. Don't trust this woman.

In MUSIQUE, unabashedly
gay, plump, queer okay,
but gay better, not afraid of
stereotypes, self-harm, self-
blame, booze, drugs, it's fine.
Who cares? Life is beautiful.

GASCON RIVES
Famous bulldog before
Gaga's bulldogs were
famous. French. Confident,
not overly friendly, however.
Sure of who he is. Doesn't
need the gig but obliges.

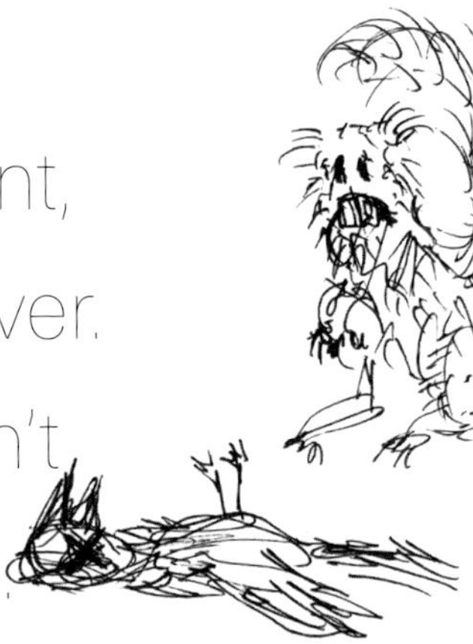

Oh, Guilt and Shame is what I meant, he said, clinking his spoon to mix sugar into his tea, over and over. He was beginning to bother me. Well, I don't want them here, I said from my bed. I looked at my body, feeling it was the body of a lowly person. He caught me with his eye.

Are you going to snatch me? I said.

He laughed his skeleton laugh.

You really worked on that cackle, I said, now quite annoyed.

Guilt and Shame are lovely ladies. They are sexy and bold. They steal money and time. They fit. You should get to know them. They enjoy the smell of their own bodies, unlike you. You'll miss it, he said, ruffling the surface of his tea through breath without a tongue.

You'll miss the subtle odors, the sublime . . .

SECURITY TEACHES A LESSON

Starring
CHARACTER

Axe is for Anxiety, for the feeling of “You don’t belong” crammed against “Hey wait a minute, I’m not trying to sell you nothing. I’m just looking for the door.”

Here we take up the actor. The actor is security, a ghost who smears himself across the vision of perfectly nice people to claim them as his victims for his, his creators, two artists in the business of telling us what we already suspect. He is a disruption. We smell open toilet stalls as he approaches.

CHARACTER emerges from the restroom, wipes hands on trouser legs, then sides of face. Slicks back hair, tugs at the edge of his uniform jacket. Begins brisk walk. Pauses. Smiles. Sniffs. Clears throat. Looks wide-eyed at the viewer. Walks. Stops. Clears throat. Smiles. Sniffs. Clears throat. Puts hands up. Sweats. Laughs. Stops. Laughs, innocent, nervous, no harm.

Bob Kil: The performance consists of repetitive minimal gestures. Three dancers and I will ride Nina Beier's readymade life-sized marble lions: gliding living bodies against the lifeless, in perfect coordination. The suggestive movements eventually meet the various verbal sounds such as gasps, shouts, etc., in sync.

The performance will be delivered daily, with the premise that the initial piece will shape-shift over time. Throughout the exhibition, I plan to converse, access, and rehearse closely with the dancers, mirroring the concept of the exhibition. Starting in February, the performance may organically evolve into a very different one by May. As for the length of the performance, it could be ten to fifteen minutes each time. Short and intense, I imagine.

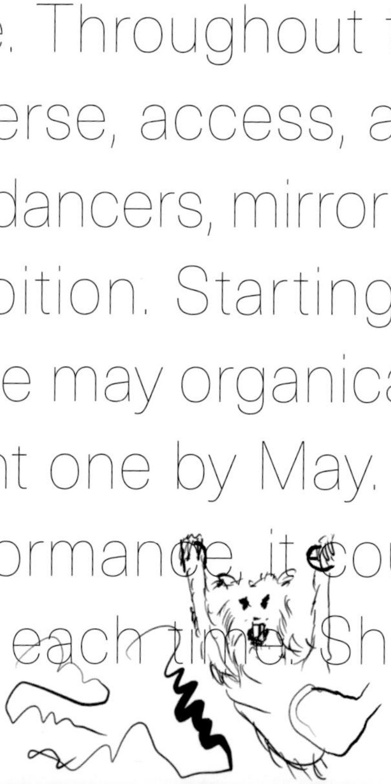

ram Moshayedi: What interests me in this ne of work is that feeling of disconnection nat occurs in the space of the exhibition, ather than one where I am made to feel omplete and whole by the experience of oking at art.

In the service of this project, I'm imagining scenario of unstable ground, where any and l propositions are able to exist within a field f plurality and their meaning is undergoing hange. Their relationship or proximity to ach and every other contribution is unstable, o that the relationships are always changing, nd meaning is always therefore in flux. This n't so much about a lack of generosity but ather a way to communicate that meaning s contingent on the presence of others, and nis may in fact preclude the need to prioritize viewer as being integral to this relationship.

CHARACTER

Hey. Hi. Yeah, yeah. So um. I get it. Believe me, I get it. I totally get it. It's like, no, dude. No, no, no. Dude. I-I-I don't want another museum security guard to tell me nothing. Okay? No, I'm not here for that. Listen, I'm here for the restrooms, for the air conditioning, see what I'm saying? I don't need a lesson from some actor dude playing security—you know what I'm saying? So, yeah, no, I'm not that.

Please. Please try and hear me out.

I am an actor. True. Yes. I'm here trying to make a living. I'm not here trying to sell you flowers, nothing like that. No phone cards—ha ha. Remember that, CDs?—with nothing on 'em too, you know what I mean?—no funerals—nothing like that. At the same time, the same time, I am an angel. Whoa—stop right there!—He he he he—

CHARACTER removes a wad of wet index cards from his breast pocket, glances at them quickly.

CHARACTER

Says actor laughs like Deputy Dog. Okay. No one knows what that means. So, no, I'm not doing that.

Pause. Beat.

CHARACTER

I'm so freaking upset. I'm upset right now. That I have to keep laughing like this. He he he he he he. It's a humiliation. I don't want to, but it's my paycheck. Understand?

You back away. CHARACTER follows.
Wipes hands on cards.

CHARACTER

I am not hokey. I'm not the one to be hokey. They call me up, this actor, right, and I say, Yeah, but is it gonna be hokey? And they assure me, they assure me, the two artists. They calm me down. They say, No, brother, it's not like that. It's real. This is a real deal. This is a museum. They don't let hokey shit in. Shit's got to be approved. This is where you get to show your talents, like who you are. I'm like, Yeah, but are any of these people willing to touch me? Are they willing? Because without that, case closed. Know what I'm saying? I cannot and will not.

You try to engage. You feel mild anxiety about your shoulders, a breathlessness.

Adam Linder: In the performing arts, I'v experienced this role of the dramaturg, whic I think typically is the person that knows th text and seeks to fulfill the veracity of th text. But as it has transpired in contemporar practice, it can be many things: it can b a theoretical researcher; it can be the kin of person who takes care of the relation dynamic within the working environment.

Fahim Amir: One idea we had was to com back to certain mythologies and myths i the context of aesthetics. How we though about it was through the Wagneria approach to the *Gesamtkunstwerk*. Richar Wagner was always thinking his work were for future audiences—a humanit that does not yet exist. So, on the one hand

'e want to propose something for a future
udience—what is the audience that's not
et there? And the other, the idea of some
nd of structural and social change.

Iolland Andrews: Sarah Vaughan's voice
. magenta with a vaporous halo of golden
ght surrounding it. It is this way because
holds your body, like you walked past a
ower you have never seen before, but its
ense of preciousness feels universal. I've
een feeling opalescent black lately. My
ar was just stolen last week. I have stolen
spects of personalities that impressed me

Andros Zins-Browne: With Fahim
mir's text, I started thinking a lot about

CHARACTER

They say nothing. The two artists. They say nothing. They look like, okay, we're gonna go in another direction. When they say that, it means you're fired—oh, I'm rambling? I am? Like milk and cheese is rambling? Like feeding my baby is rambling? You didn't think I had a youngster? Oh, yeah. I do. I do. I need the job, and you're thinking what's this motherfucker going on about? Oh, I'm sorry, but that's what they wrote. See. It says right here. Says—holding index card out shakily—to viewer. Viewer. That's you. You view. I speak. You view. I kid you not. It says this right here.

Let me collect myself.

CHARACTER sniffs, smooths his hair, clears his throat, shifts his stance. You have no choice.

CHARACTER They say nothing. This is when I bring my skill set in. Why don't I perform a miracle? Okay? I'll perform a miracle. At this point, I talk about how I can lift souls. Like with my body, with my mind, with my existence, my thoughts. And they were like, Yeah, but can you, like, lift your . . . can you stand on your—can you lift your body up with one hand, like, more like a stunt, like gymnastics? I say, Certainly.

CHARACTER lifts his body up, standing on one hand, up into the air.

CHARACTER They say, can you walk toward, say, a visitor, as though holding your body aloft. I say, Certainly.

Jumps back to an upright position.

CHARACTER They say, Can you account for your time on this planet? I say, Certainly. They say, Can you fix yourself in time? I say, I cannot, because I am the experience. I am the matter. I am the now. And then I'm gone.

chameleons. The question "What color a chameleon?" felt potent, as I considere theft as an act of communing and of (sel expression. Choreographically, I imagine working with a performer to morp between several bodies, establishing prototypically male performative in th vein of Benito Mussolini to deliver what understood from Fahim would be a kind c political speech, but that would abstrac dissolve, and code switch.

Holland Andrews: Hunted is dar brown; brass is played; daffodil yellow i transmitting; red and yellow like a mang is ambush; olive green is wanting; *miel* is glimmer; spacious p i n k is seen; pal blue, like blue on a planet that was mad f water but is now ice, is thirst; amethyst i hear you; faded lilac is going; mossy rick keeps coming; red is lasting; blush promise; neon orange is threat; clear nidnight sky is water . . .

ahim Amir: I would have to only insist n a very strict keeping to the script. This till leaves much room for arrangements, ounterinterpretations of the production eam, and still could give it a totally different neaning from what I personally envisioned. And in this context this would be okay vith me. But, every change of words in ny extent would have to be rechecked vith me. No matter what much-cherished Roland Barthes may have written, this author" isn't dead yet.

M/OM

Starring
COMEDIAN and CHARACTER

Mother and Child (M/OM) have a day out. Mother should be played by COMEDIAN, The Most Fake of All Aging Has-Beens. Child should be played by CHARACTER, My Multiple Selves Stuffed into an Economy-Sized Lip-Tube called Body. In the course of our dance, we shall reveal our bald heads, fringes of curly hair, our emotional dyslexia. Resentments dominate. Love takes the form of an injection, "I can do this to you . . ."

The dance begins after M/OM have watched too much television and gestured and tapped on a window from inside a moving vehicle to select the perfect parking spot, which they have changed too many times, after having bickered about the directions for a childproof cap, after complaining about the cold, about the food, after debating the genetics of a hare as seen in an old film of an old artist who tried to help us, who tried, tried, and failed.

CHARACTER — It's more of a feeling, I said, gesturing. I feel it.

COMEDIAN — Yes, but be specific, Marvin—

CHARACTER — My mother said, clipping her nails. She's in love with Anderson Cooper, by the way. She can't stop talking about him.

COMEDIAN — Anderson Cooper.

CHARACTER — How do you make a sign for an exasperated exhale?

I ask my body, Right Leg, Right Leg, who's in there?

Well, said Right Leg, It's your inability to move forward, tied to your anger, tied to your heart, tied to the inflammation in the blood vessels of your Brain.

Oh, I said, Out of resentment, out of unrelenting pain?

She's also in love with Warren Buffett, her hero. My hero, she says, as I dab her lips with a rag. She's always talking 'bout Warren.

COMEDIAN — He could have done anything with his money.

CHARACTER — I tell her of my misfortune, my loss of will, my impotence, my failure to love—

COMEDIAN — Ah, I had that.

CHARACTER — My mother says.

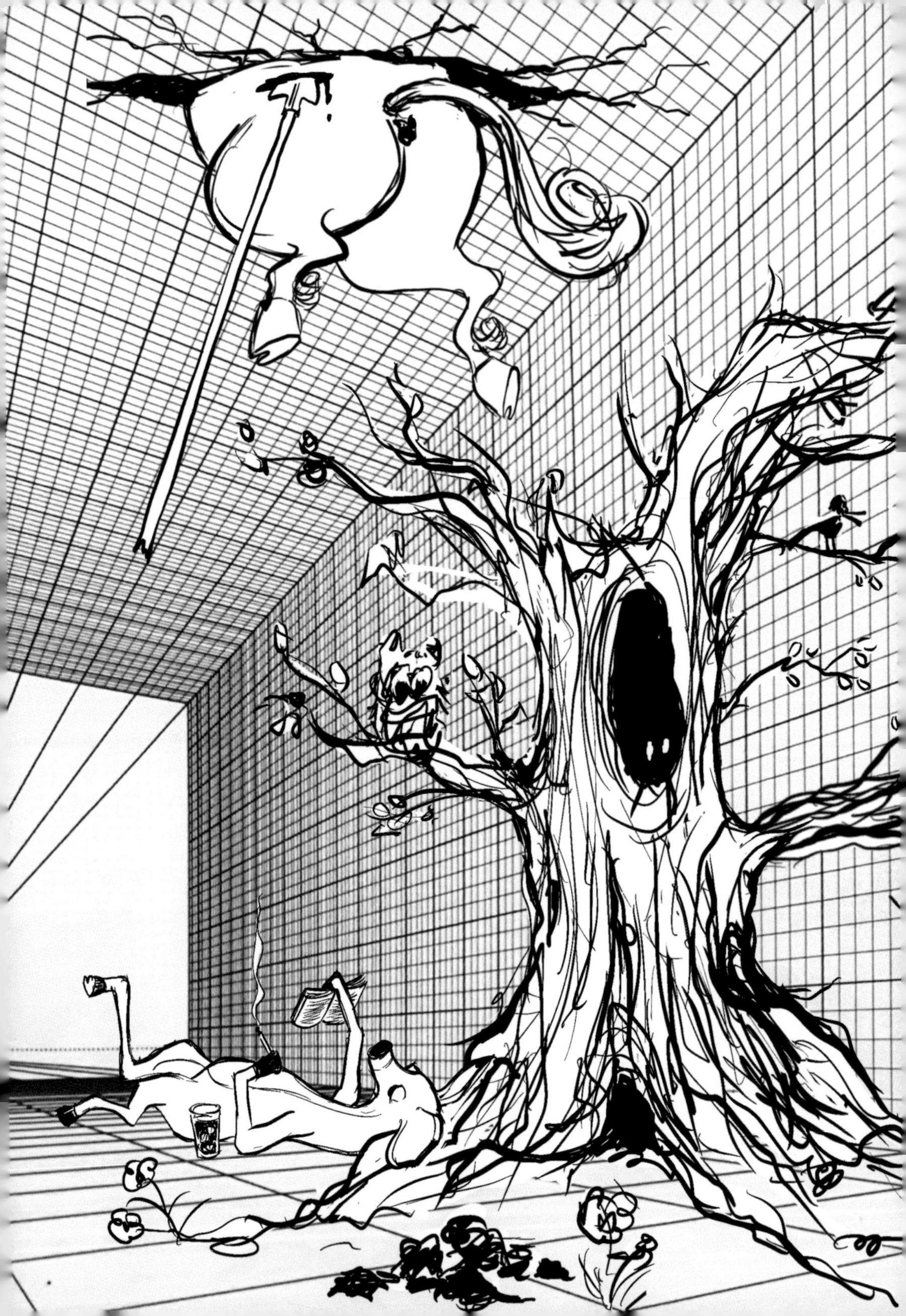

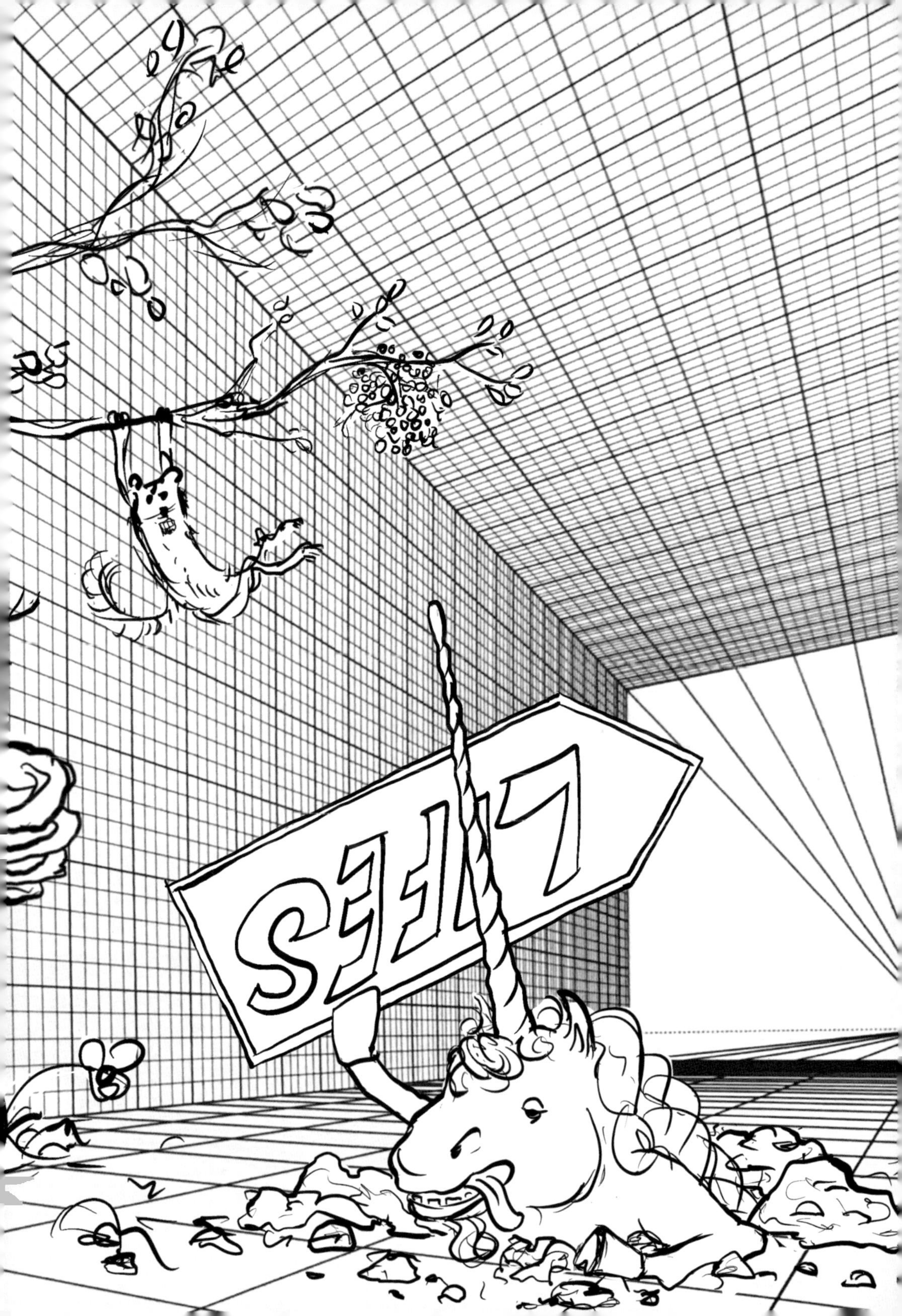
LIES

COMEDIAN	I had that as a child, as a product of a harsh society.
CHARACTER	You did not.
COMEDIAN	I did. I'm telling you.
CHARACTER	You cannot possibly have my disease.
COMEDIAN	Why not?
CHARACTER	Because it is mine. It's my disease.
COMEDIAN	Well, it could be spreading.
CHARACTER	You just told me you had it. *Had* is past tense.
COMEDIAN	Well, I said it was chronic.
CHARACTER	You did *not.*
COMEDIAN	I said it was in an advanced state, and now it's chronic.

CHARACTER and COMEDIAN shift their affect. They establish a rhythm.

CHARACTER	I mean, I'm stumped. I'm thoroughly stumped. How should you get my disease in the ten minutes we've been standing here?
COMEDIAN	Are you listening to me? It's killing me.
CHARACTER	I told you. I'm sick. I'm ill.
COMEDIAN	With what? With what are you ill?

CHARACTER	With rage, I'm sick. I am in an advanced state of your sneaky, insidious rage, and now I am riddled with rancor. Look—are you trying to get money out of me?
COMEDIAN	No. How much do you have?
CHARACTER	I have a dollar, one dollar. I told you I'm poor. I'm impoverished.
COMEDIAN	But you're standing in an edifice
CHARACTER	In a what?
COMEDIAN	An edifice, a testament, a monument. You pass. Listen, I'll take that dollar. Let me see your purse.
CHARACTER	I don't carry a purse.
COMEDIAN	(Reaching) Let me see it.
CHARACTER	(Clutching) It's my last money. It's all I have.
COMEDIAN	I'm sure your friends at the door will help you.
CHARACTER	They are not my friends!
COMEDIAN	They are! They are the force, the force, the force, the powers that be. They stand before the longest, fastest boulevard in the West, the most notable, the most often depicted in films and television, broadcast along shores of countries you can't even dream about, and you tell me you don't have

Jessika Kenney: We could make a music composition based on each example tha is pretty simple, so we could all just learn and do it, and I think taking out the words really cool, and then just extracting a line o even a mode or even a vocal timbre or colo then we can identify what that thing is an make it a group composition, and we cou all teach each other about different thing we hear in that example. Like we each brin one piece, and we create one fragment fo each of those pieces. Which of (the many you(s) is in or not in this performance (o how you relate to these fragments)?

Kite: I see the museum as a place of powe that wields power, and I can only hope t borrow a fraction of that power to gai onetary and cultural capital in order to transfer it back to my people, who are not elcome in such spaces ever.

I think I'm coming from a place of erformance, of making art as a gift to elations (settler or Indigenous) who may or ay not love you back. You get the gift, you ve the gift, regardless. If all performance a gift, can it be a vicious gift?

DEOLOGICAL APPARATUS

ahim Amir: *Gift* means *poison* in German nyways. So, it's always both.

Ultra Ultra ULTRA
Soft Gentle STRONG

indon Johnson: We definitely want to equest the four to five tons of soapstone as n offering to L. Frank, and we also want to sk for access to the Catalina Chimes for a

power? You tell me you are ill on marble quarried from Italy and in part Poland? Henchmen would give their left nuts to stand here with you, and you tell me you don't have a dollar bill to give your own mother? Drive yourself to shame, to shame, to shame!

Beat.

CHARACTER I can't stand it.

COMEDIAN He has everything and now he can't stand.

CHARACTER The whole thing, you, your actions, your affect, your accent, your aura, your effusions.

COMEDIAN But you're a supplicant, a lover, a licker of boots, a slovenly craven crouch.

CHARACTER An applicant.

COMEDIAN A penitent.

CHARACTER So?

COMEDIAN And?

CHARACTER What do you want me to do about it?

COMEDIAN Sell the rights.

CHARACTER To what?

COMEDIAN Anything! Make it up.

CHARACTER	You?
COMEDIAN	To me?
CHARACTER	Yes, you. The rights. Are they up for grabs?
COMEDIAN	(Winking) I'm always up for grabs.
CHARACTER	(Romantically, earnestly) May I kiss you? May I deepen our wealth?
COMEDIAN	Yes. Like snakes in mouths, like poisoned tips, like Laocoön, or whatthefuckshisname we can never pronounce, like ominous swarms, the Holy Cross blocking the sun, like the display bones of a once gargantuan tiger, the lapping of shores, of animatronic bees flirting with holographic flowers, yes, yes, yes! As in Paul Simon's "Mother and Child Reunion," we shall never be free until we are One.
CHARACTER	May I place myself in you now?
COMEDIAN	Why certainly. Of course.
CHARACTER	May I complete the Biblical task of incorporation?
COMEDIAN	With flourish, with flair!
CHARACTER	May I fuse the double helix of desire?
COMEDIAN	Go 'head.
CHARACTER	May I pen you in?
COMEDIAN	At once.

three-month long intervention but no nee yet to commit/comment on the possibili of L. Frank's composition, as it could b that she wants to go in another directio However, either way, the chimes will be useful material for us. We haven't spoke about the chimes yet to L. Frank, we wante to give her a gift first.

Cooper Jacoby: Stemming from this, wondered how could I engage UCLA Multisensory Processing Lab in a way tha doesn't just reproduce the status quo of certain Instagram type of "immersive ar and moves past the elementary "high pitc noise = nervous; warm light = calming" kin of conclusions. I kept returning to the ide of how déjà vu could be triggered, how it uttering in time and that uncanny feeling f familiarity could be choreographed. While some ways it's a bit boilerplate sci-fi, but what if the memory or specific feeling of amiliarity was a data set, a scripted memory hat is choreographed to feel familiar through certain set of visual, textual, audio, thermal ueues? What if it was a memory co-written y AI?

Or put another way: Could a specific eeling or memory be generated, subliminally oded in a specific choreography of erceptual or attention cues and then evealed?

Nicholas Barlow: Aram Moshayedi and I ave had many conversations about the egacy of Institutional Critique and the

CHARACTER	May I halt this rocking parade of cultural tools?
COMEDIAN	Naturally.
CHARACTER	And shimmy on the ground on hairy all fours?
COMEDIAN	*Mais oui!* But of course!
CHARACTER	As signified by a curse?
COMEDIAN	As seen on TV.
CHARACTER	As previewed in a crystal skull.
COMEDIAN	In a teardrop.
CHARACTER	In a microbead!
COMEDIAN	In a dead dog's eye!
CHARACTER	And after, we'll eat?
COMEDIAN	With open mouths.
CHARACTER	Closely, a foamy bubble between.
COMEDIAN	And parking!
CHARACTER	Free parking.
COMEDIAN	In a city of love, a city of slippery dreams.

There follows an embrace. Let's be frank. Who knows what lurks in pronouncements of knowledge, of incestual pie throwing and naked, slithery complications?

ALL RIGHT, SO BRING IT BACK

Starring
PORN STAR

Okay, porn stars, right? Respectable profession. Healthy. The gay stars, especially. Cut, manicured, programmers by day, heavy "likes" on the platforms, geographers, Vloggers, horticulturists, Sanskrit scholars, nice. Still, one can't help the feeling that, here in the collection, when one is seated on a custom plaster bench, a custom towel draped discreetly over one's form-fitting designer shorts, one is involved in a subtler exchange. PORN STAR, a good boy, beefy, shredded, attracts. His dance is a dialogue. He speaks nervously, making convo, keeping the ball rolling, answering the obvious, anticipating his interviewer's commands. INTERVIEWER is invisible, insistent, smart. For PORN STAR, this is a paid gig. Parking validated. Voucher for lunch. All you can eat, no refills.

strangeness of having archival materi represent it in a museum exhibition. It is gesture to the past, to spaces a viewer n longer has access to—artwork drained c its intended meaning and specificity, arrivin at the museum as a dead object. In ou conversations, in thinking about how we'r going to address the museum, in respons to this lineage, that's been a real issue—t not engage with dead presences.

Olivia Mole: I've thought through this ide of a mascot, an intermediary, commentato metatext, etc., and the book as a paralle virtual space of the museum.

It seems appropriate for me to brin characters from across these differen existing projects, because they have alread een emptied of their original cultural roles, ses, and to different extents, their original ppearances. They are also drawn from arious instances of a cultural relationship to nature," which is, I think, in keeping with the xhibition's texts and concerns. So it would e a motley crew of, say, a unicorn, Bambi, keletor, Charmin bear, a cosplay tree, a worm, lairball Omphalos, primitive cube-heads, an nnamable god-cloud, etc. Not necessarily ll of them but enough such that they read s a rolling collective. Specific to the context f this show, I have, at least in my head, come think of this ensemble as "the Lowlifes" like that it sounds like a sitcom or garage and, as well as that they inhabit a kind of ndercarriage version of the "proper" show the formal galleries. (Hopefully surfacing the toilets!) Though, like any infestation,

PORN STAR

There are, uh, lots of, uh, people from other planets around here. I didn't say people from other plants, did I? I get nervous. I don't wanna say the wrong thing. People from other planets smoke a lot. Notice that? They're chain smokers. I read that too. What's the point? What's the point is that you're getting to know me. My thoughts.

PORN STAR takes his shirt off.

PORN STAR

Oh, yeah, three or four times a week. Yeah, I run, lift, swim on Mondays. Uh-huh. Yeah, they got a swimming pool. I go there sometimes.

PORN STAR blinks, waits for the question.

PORN STAR

As far as being a tranny? I'm not though. So I can't comment on that.

Rods. That's Biblical, that's where you turn a snake into a staff, I'm thinking. People at Costco? Oh, man that shit is crazy. The lines. People go nuts. Oh, flex? Sure.

PORN STAR flexes an expensive bicep. An imaginary curl.

PORN STAR

The post office too. How this one lady—okay, this could be delicate. I don't want to put anybody down, but she got so mad at the post office, talking about how this Korean lady didn't give her the right change. Yeah, it's true, she was a white lady, and we were all, like, tone it down and don't be a, well, you know. But she wasn't embarrassed at all. In fact, she made the woman count her change over and over. Everyone in line was shifting, like getting tired of this bullshit and rolling their eyes. I had a friend like that. He would demand that his coffee be made at 180 degrees. He doesn't get respect, I guess. In his mind. People love him. They do. They outright love him. But he doesn't see it. So he takes it out on service people, you know.

His brows furrow. Huh?

PORN STAR

Me? A service person? Ha. No. No.

He gets back to it, smoking.

PORN STAR

I get really entranced by the shape of an alien head, you know. Like *The Scream*, like from this artist, this artist of the twentieth century.

Oh, take it out? Sure.

A pleasant surprise.

they could end up anywhere, even in space they're not supposed to be.

NEW WAYS OF BEING, IN THE ABANDONNED ASSET FIELDS

Cooper Jacoby: I imagine the work existin in the Infrathin and as a series of reactior based on heat, atmosphere, and proximit At the core of this assembly is a series c thermostats which relay temperature an humidity, while using these inputs and the slight variations to determine the mood c an ongoing, AI-generated narrative which displayed on a screen. When temperature shift toward dry and cool, a melancholi data set drives the tone; when readings ar hotter and more humid, an altruistic data se feeds the script. The narrative prompt th devices repeatedly ask themselves is: Hov will I survive?

ndon Johnson: ~~We had a really nice chat day about ways to make the text feel more elevant and intertwined with the ideas we e having. We're gonna send it back through e algorithm process with two of the original ison papers, the transcript from the film *ngel's Egg* (very relevant), the transcript om the film *Bacurau* (also relevant), the anscript from the bison tour we took on the land, and a paper on invasive plant species Catalina. We also wanted to add the script om the film *The Vanishing American*, which the film that they brought the buffalo to imu for. Once we've got the script for *The anishing American*, I think it will take us bout two weeks to come up with a really ood more idk relevant piece of writing. What e're looking for in one way or another is a urationally substantive but not linear thing.~~

PORN STAR We're in the twenty-first century, though, like well into it.

PORN STAR glances at his towel.

PORN STAR Oh, thanks. I like it too. Yeah. Of course. How will it be? Like in history? Oh, man, I think it'll be a mixed bag. Like how we are, um, I dunno, you know, in some respects lost as a species and in some respects very empathetic, you know, in love with life, feeling into the non-human much, much more, much more than we used to. Non-human. Ha. That's a fucked up phrase. Yeah? Uh-huh.

An anticipated task.

PORN STAR Like, um, oh, man—ha ha—it's hard to do two things at the same time. Notice that? It's hard to talk and—uh—but I've got it down, I think. Yeah.

What I like? Oh, uh. For sure. Um.

Paris, France. Hands down. The Pompidou. I'd wanna go.

Best in show?

PORN STAR Hm. Monet, I guess.

For the online issue:

PORN STAR Weirdest? Oh, Japanese toilets, for sure. Ha ha.

Ha. Huh? Oh, *Goodfellas*, I guess. Yeah.

Whole Foods salad bar, hands down. Load up on those micronutrients. Kick a little mashed potatoes in there on the side.

Clicks teeth, laughs, then, almost inaudible.

PORN STAR Buttery.

Kevin. Yeah, Kevin. Yeah, definitely Kevin.

And so SHE comes around a corner, like right on your ass, all of a sudden.

~~Suzanne Kite got an awesome lea~~
~~about the kelp through Nick Shapiro a~~
~~UCLA. Their team seems awesome, an~~
~~I bet they'll be able to help us figure ou~~
~~our questions about kelp materially an~~
~~give us more background. Do you thin~~
~~Nicholas Barlow can get the ball rolling fo~~
~~us with them? Suzanne's contact suggeste~~
~~speaking with Maura Palacios Mejia i~~
~~particular.~~

Morag Keil: i had an idea and wanted to shar
cause could be a kind of large undertakin
re: production. i was thinking along th
puke lines and the tubes. to have a see
thru tube system that puke-like substanc
flows throughout the gallery. how does thi
sound? do u think its possible?

ora Budor: I also spoke to Morag Keil nce more, to see if we could do something gether, but it seems like we won't see each her in Tbilisi, and it may be too complicated dding another level of distancing to the ork process . . . Thus, I have a proposal at could work, taking into consideration e remoteness and time.

I was concerned with how to create nother presence, or another space in the now by using an absence of sorts. Reading ahim Amir's book was generative (and ome online rants about removal of the rport smoking cabins in L.A.): *"The more olluted we feel to ourselves, the more we ish for something edifying, something pure, y which we can pull ourselves to full height."* his is a very Bataillean thought, indeed; in Musée," Georges Bataille discusses a double

IN THE SPIRIT OF SAYING THINGS TWICE

Starring
OBVIOUSLY FEMALE

Now look, viewer, look here, I am not the one. I am not the one to be soothing your woes, I am not the one to be twisting my ankle on your "The customer is always right" nonsense. The customer is . . . what? What if you were at my place. Huh? You'd say, Why don't you help your granny? Why don't you clean up this mess? Whose bra is this? Is this your bra? Get what I'm saying? I am not the help. Don't call me mean. Call me dumb. Call me Groped at the Cocktail Bar. Call me No One Bought My Book. Call me I Thought I Was Better than This and Look I Broke My Heel. Jeez. This is a dance of You and Me, your pain, my pain, your unwillingness to see me, and my resentment of you as I attempt, god knows why, to cure your ills. God knows why, coz your ills are incurable, Boss. You love me? Oh, you do? Well, shit. Now we can talk. Now you can have my baby. Now I can give you what I need.

OBVIOUSLY FEMALE

I dip, I move, I shake my ass, I fly about the room.

Violence, I say to my soul, as I dip and carve and careen when this old dude comes in looking for the parking lot. I look at him like he's out of his mind, and he is. I'm like, Why would you park your car on the second floor of a goddamn museum, a goddamn space of culture?

He looks at me with tears in his eyes. He's like, I lost my wife. I'm like: So?

His tears begin, ya know, rolling down his cheeks. He pouts and reaches his hands out to me sorta half, sorta, half limp, like a baby, like a sad baby. He wants me to jump into those arms. I say, Well. You married her. You chose her.

He steps back. He looks at me, like, You monster, you devil, you bat outta hell. He shakes his head. He had the nerve to check his ticket. Now just who do you think I am? I'd like to do for you something special. This is the metal hinge on the trap door. When I say it's all too much for me, I mean it.

bind between the slaughterhouse and th museum, and their flows of production ar consumption: "A museum is like the lungs of great city; the crowd floods into the museu every Sunday like blood and it leaves purifie and fresh."

He also reminds us that th slaughterhouses are the negative pole, th generator of repulsion, the centrifuge (the are placed farther and farther away fro the center of the city)—unlike museums, th pole of attraction, are centripetal. But withi the heart of one the other is hidden.

Consider the museum itself a plac of unproductive expenditure (satisfactio without loss, pleasure without labor); place where we come to purify ourselve (as if it were possible to spend and be sper without getting dirty).

Smoking—"*a pleasure one gives neself through the ingestive channel that closest to auto-affection; the voice or rality*" (Jacques Derrida). There is also an ssociation between burning and the ruin of nemory, a destructive aspect to the heat that ses up through the floor, to the flared match nd the burning tip of the cigarette. The term so carries connotations of preservation; ust as smoking preserves meat and fish r future consumption, tobacco smoking is way of preserving the past. It's an aspect f history slowly becoming a curiosity, a gnifier of lower or creative class.

Isn't this also one of the things that nuseums do, preserve history? In the rchives, on the walls and the pedestals vorks stand, sanitized, extracted from the onditions of their making.

I am not made for this world. Not built for it. I am built for the call of the blue jay, the shrike, the shifting of dry leaves 'neath a cat's hunting paw, sunshine, the waiting, the waiting . . .

What I want to do is give you love. Trouble is, I don't know you. See what I'm saying?

She stops, saunters, looks about.

OBVIOUSLY FEMALE What kind of place is this? Huh?

I let out a gas.

I hop. I jerk. I stand on one leg.

I step. I parade. I wave my arms gently, light enough to show the wobble. Light, light, like scratching a baby's back.

Now feel me.

Have you ever been a victim, just picking at your meal? Well, it happened to me. I set forth a tirade, an animal in my speech. A rager, said the old man. Said, Well, you present yourself as a lucky charm, as a modified interlocutor with centuries of vulgar, shrieking pain.

I do?

He took two fingers out, two trying to jab me in my breastbone, armed as he was with his solitary love.

I said: Now there you go. That's honesty. That's the crybaby's truth right there.

And he broke. And I broke. And we broke broke broke. And we broke up. We broke down. We broke up, all around, until we were tired, fired, exhausted.

See? See what I'm trying to say? See?

I proceed to talk to the walls, to the banisters, to mumble to the doorknobs till I make my case, till the walls crumble, till the threads bounce, till the roots pull up and walk back home.

And just as naturally, she swoops out. Wow, what a danger she is, what a pill, what a wrong turn. And here she comes hauling back.

The elimination of smoking (as we as factory smoke, incinerators, chimne and grill smoke) from the city corresponc to the image of a thriving Western cit characterized by its absence . . .

Chastised over the last years as a almost immoral activity, smoking provide an illustrative example of a biopolitica tactic. In this work, it is preserved in it museological format.

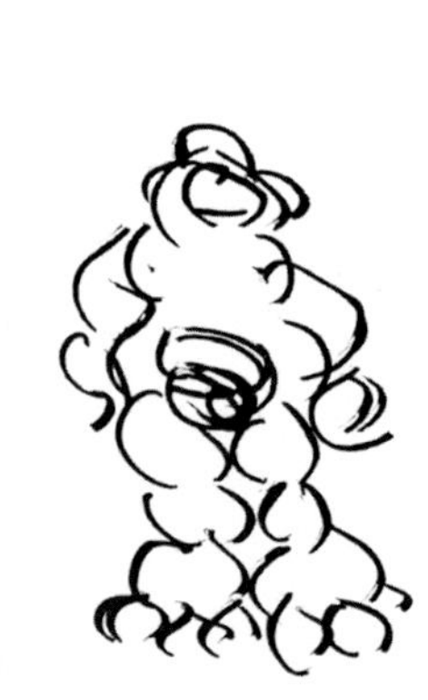

Un chant d'amour, 2021
Synthetic cigarette smell
dispersed at random intervals.

Few notes: the smell is artificial, a syntheti mimic of cigarette smoke odor. A bit of ngering cigarette smoke, one that sits in e air. A visitor walking through perceives it some point. It transports them elsewhere; erhaps confuses; it's the *50 cc of Paris Air*, ut of an unwanted social nature. *Un chant 'amour* might be too much of an homage— ut then again I love that film so much.

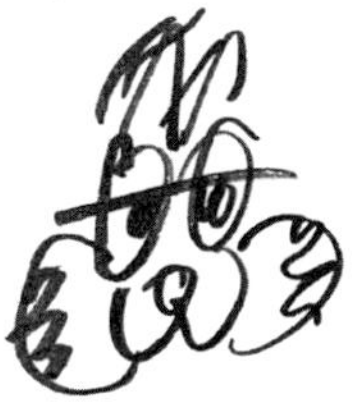

Morag Keil: Puke – a recipe (small):

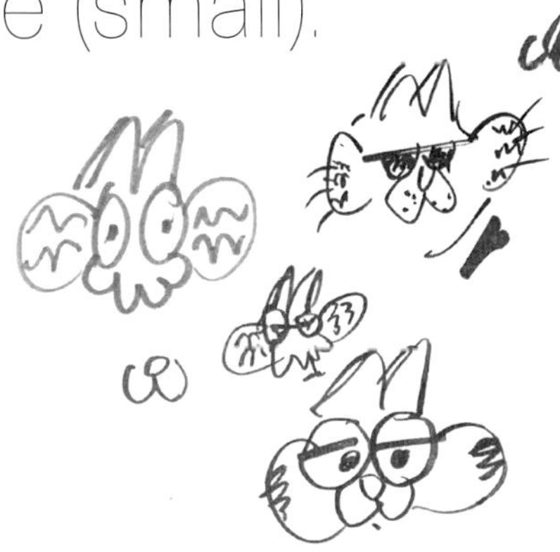

2 x kiwi fruit

1 bag fresh spinach

Handful of fresh cranberries

1/2 x iceberg lettuce

Double or triple recipe for larger quantities.

ANIMAL REGRET

Starring
OBVIOUSLY FEMALE

In this vehicle, I, OBVIOUSLY FEMALE, tote a bag. I got those shoes. My shorts ride the crack. I'm old as fuck. I talk on the phone. I ignore you. I let my body taunt. This is my story. My Truth! This is my repulse of the skinny, of the dead, of the rational, of the attenuated, hard, never alleviated heart.

OBVIOUSLY FEMALE

(Into the phone) They said, He's so fine, you won't regret.

I walked.

To the beat. To the beat. To the be-be-be—beat. I dropped the beat like this. Like—uh.

Sssh.

They said, Eyeballs. They said, Looks.

They said, L-l-l-l-looks.

Animals in 5K. Said, Uh.

When can a man be a fur daddy, like a revenge mink, like a staple gun with dead eyes, like a, uh? I said, Uh. I said, enunciating the *what do you want* part.

They said, I need you to be stare-able, fixable, traceable, like a finger in a grease hole. So. I said. Why not?

Who comes to a space like this 'less there's a Pop-Tart at the end? Caller, you say what?

Let me tell you about my—five six seven eight—okay, well, I called up Spectrum, said, what? I called up AT&T, said, I didn't make these calls. Betty says, Obviously you did, Ma'am, coz the numbers are on your bill. I said, Are you working from home, because I can hear your dog. Said, Well, matter of fact, he's right here. Hold the phone. Dog says, You

Cooper Jacoby: What is the set temperatu of the gallery? Do you know if there's a s range at which it fluctuates or if the settir changes?

Nicholas Barlow: 70-degree temp with + 3 degree allowance. 50% relative humidi with +/- 8% allowance.

Cooper Jacoby: Michael Monaha mentioned that staff sometimes gets ema reports about the change of temperatur in the galleries. Who receives these email and how are they generated?

Nicholas Barlow: The Siemens BMS syster

HVAC controller) generates an email if the system is out of range. Hammer Security also patrols to check on gallery devices. Hammer Security, Portland McCormick (Director of Registration and Collections Management), building engineers, and Henry Clancy (Director of Operations) receive the alerts.

ram Moshayedi: I talked to Dannielle Sergent from Cognoscenti about the synthetic cigarette smell, and she raised some issues to consider. Cold diffusion vs. hot diffusion: which scent dispersion method is best? Also, natural ingredients have more allergens than synthetics. She says the subtler the better, the nose can perceive a small fraction of smell over great distances. For acrid old cigarette smell, she

and me, you and me. Over and over again. Like in my mouth. I says, You better slow down. Dog says, The whole thing is a classical setup, a fake. Says, This is somebody's fantasy, but it ain't mine. I said, You know what, I agree with you.

Like today, I went to get my mail. All these people were standing round my box—no—they were hovering around my letters, Sir. Said, What you doing here? Said, We're spies. I said, Well, you are some pretty damn obvious spies to be hovering around my box, I mean, I can't even get to it— Said, Well, that's the point, we're reading it. Said, Well, let me see that paper. They said, You know, I'm not sure this is a real sale here over at CVS. They said, Because these Bic pens are supposed to be on sale at 3.99 from 4.25, but they've always been 3.99. I'm like, You know, they do that. They do that around the holidays when your adrenalin is high, like when your cingulate gyrus is spinning and your amygdala is pumping heat. These spies were like, Whooo! That's the gawdshonestwooth, they said, dribbling outta the sides of their mouths. When they said it like that, I knew:

Spaceships.

Star feelers.

Ant heads on dope.

The way out.

Force feeding a goblin with a long-ass spoon.

Darts in the eyes with a tennis ball.

They said, Ma'am, that's some crazy shit.

I said, You know what, you know what? That's the tempo of the times.

advised less is more. She also warned th
smells can stick around.

Rindon Johnson: Sound Work Duration–
the work is a composition that will last th
duration of the show, it will change as th
solstice gets closer and will be responsiv
to the movement of the sun. We definite
want the song to be amplified outsid
the galleries, into the courtyard and ont
the street as well. As far as predictabilit
of the sound or working with the othe
sound works, I think the issue here is tha
the work's interruptive (for lack of a bette
word) nature is one of the keys of the piec
The song's context being a children's slav
song means that it won't always be regula
but a good rule of thumb is that the son

ould be expected approximately every
teen minutes.

ora Budor: I spoke to my contact at the stitute for Art and Olfaction, Saskia Wilson-rown, and she gave me a bit of different formation!

Cigarette smoke is one of the most omplex odors, containing more than four undred types of odor molecules. I guess ere are very different approaches to making is—she said she would recommend atural infusion (which is literally something e soaking cigarette butts in infusion and en extracting it?), as she doubts that the ynthetic version would represent the smell ealistically. Unless, she said, there would e a visual cue such as a bit of smoke/fog,

MUSIQUE

Starring
COMEDIAN

COMEDIAN

Think stone walls and ivy, think papier-mâché. Think of an individual wearing a fence with vines and creepers of crisp inorganic blends of materials with scientific names. Think how lovely it is to wear a sign, to be a sign. How sexy. How free. Think passing out pamphlets in front of the museum, of indications, beliefs, of buses blocking traffic, of waiting for the next round, of what it will be like when it's all over.

COMEDIAN is everyone's fun gay, not queer gay. He's upbeat. Looks you in the eyes. You know why? He ate all the coffee cake at the office party and will vomit it up tonight. He speaks.

COMEDIAN

I had a beautiful dream about being ravaged by Musical Comedy. Yes, delightful. He wore a black blazer with silver piping, a lot of netting, and fanciful seventeenth-century, buckled shoes. He had arranged everything so that there was an easel where you could write anything you wanted—yes, anything, anything you desired—and moss grew everywhere, and there was an earthen elevator chute, which is, if you survived in—is that a phrase?—If you, uh, felled down to, felled downed into, or if you survived into it?—Well, if you fell down there and lived, you could see all these wonderful semi-comatose patients on gurneys. You could inject whomever you wanted, including Ram Dass. He offered all this. But are you going to fuck me? I said. Yes, yes, yes, of course, Musical Comedy said. Oh, I said. Good. I was worried there for a while.

###
end

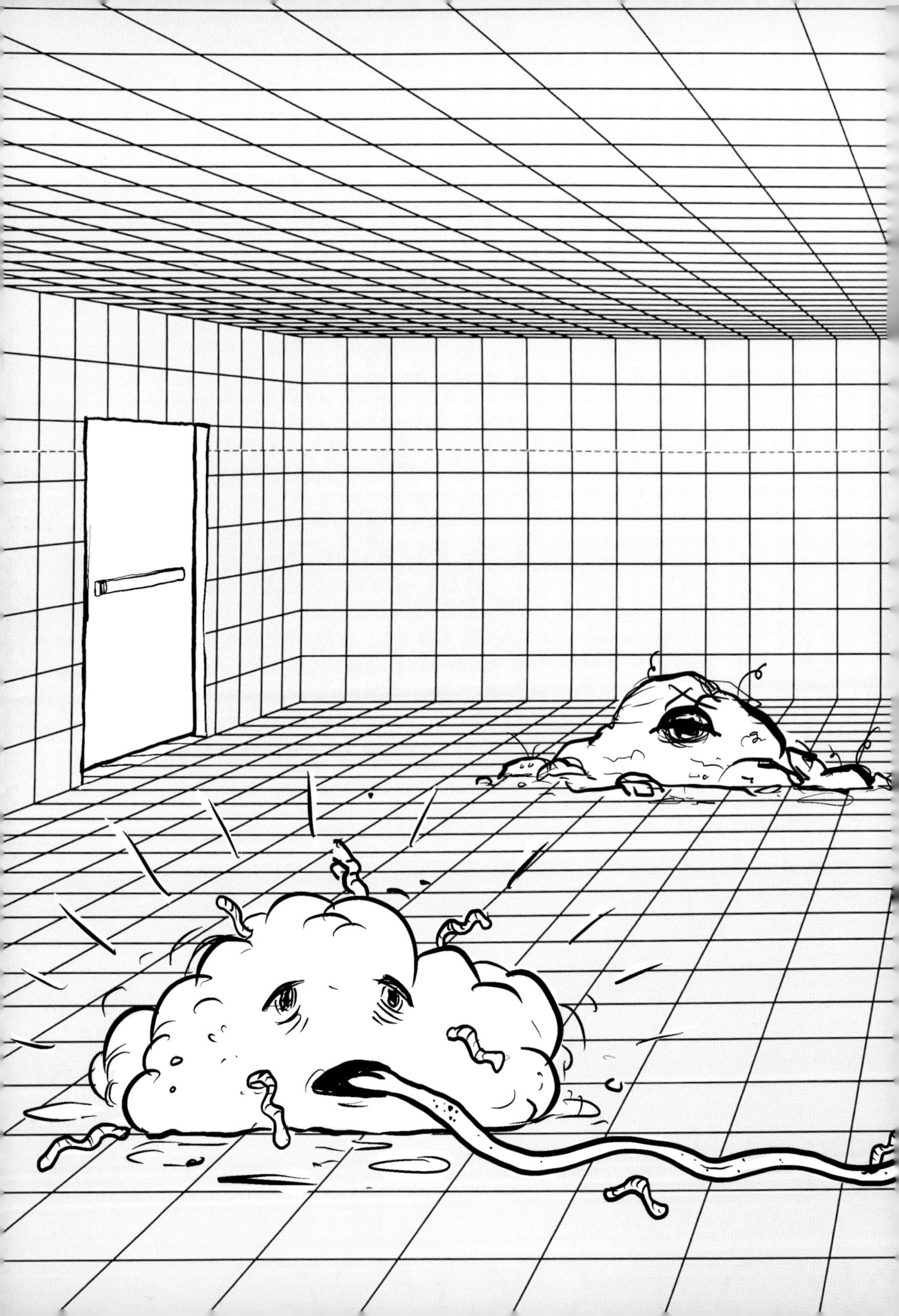

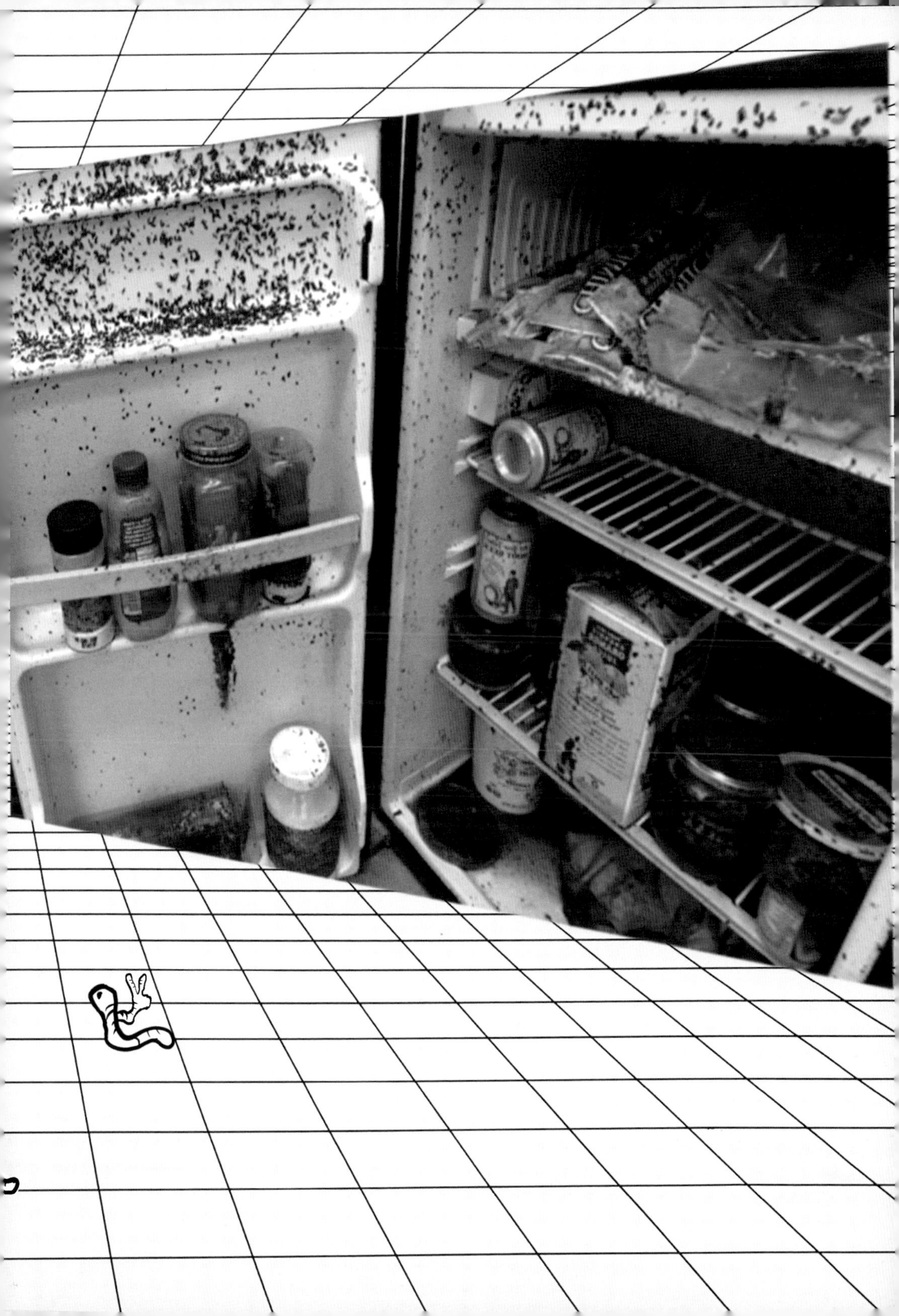

Implied in the ship is the float

(My horse is American)

RINDON JOHNSON

0 Where we ended up is far from here, but these frames are where we began.

1 First Darkness, then you nearby, and then a rising sun, every day it is like this, pushing inward and then outward. Always the same question. There's no answer, nothing to see, I've been telling you, I see aboard their crafts, there's nothing there, containers, worn bodies. What happens in the realms of men? Who was there and what roles did they play? I once heard that if you find the right one and you say the right thing, it can start chewing on their brain, order wooden mallets, shouting, hit me, please hit me. Is that right? I thought that we were building something. I've already built something. Oh. Start at the beginning then, please. Well, the light streams through and we are not hungry. I meant the story. Oh.

because the brain can apparently use it compensate for the olfactory lack. But I dor want that . . .

So it is interesting that Dannielle Serge believes this smell can be synthesized.

I think one thing to address wit Dannielle is that the smell wouldn't b present the whole time—as it would b dispersed at random intervals, thus nc "filling" the space at all times and infusing soaking into other works. As everythin in the show is timed, this piece would b timed as well, even in a way where it can b dispersed just in one area, and then lettin it diffuse naturally and disappear. It woul be good to have her advice if this versio seems potentially dangerous, or if this i something that would be fine if it is in sma amounts and at intervals.

ndon Johnson: L. Frank was very happy ith the stones I stole from Pimu and was ven happier to hear that a whole boulder as hers to choose. ~~When we asked her here she'd like the boulder, she explained at there is a cliff at Loyola Marymount niversity where the Tongva would have rge gatherings.~~ She'd like the boulder to e there so that she can teach her people e stone techniques. She said there are a w other places, but that's her first choice. bviously, we must try and make this happen.

Now that we've had such progress with e chimes, we'd like our sound work to follow e chimes' rhythm so to play every fifteen inutes, it will not be longer than a minute. here's going to be a second layer to the ound work, something that follows the lunar chedule that we're still working on.

2 There were several ways that things could have gone, and they have gone this way.

3 The reality is nobody owns that, can you see that, is that clear?

4 First, you take your hands and place them just here, don't look directly in front, and, okay, here is the blue visage, if you can just lie back not on the, just backwards, reduce towards, and there isn't a ground. I meant, there were several ways that things could have gone, and they have gone this way. There was the tide alone, and the other things, the matter, the reorganization as such, the stumbling over, on top of, as if something could form, would form, couldn't but did still, in spite of itself, or myself, or whatever, it was just us, and then some time much later, you and between us whatever we need at the time, you of course, the sower, the fisherman, the crook, the thief, a shaft of something, I could hear it, or whatever hearing meant at that time, a great buoyancy, full and emptying and filling again. Gifts.

~~I wish we could speak more direct about the kelp, it will definitely be connecte and feel that way, as I'm working throug the text I feel like the kelp's presence w be connected.~~

Dora Budor: In the meantime, I also asked Ti McClintock, a scientist from the Universi of Kentucky who seems to have created la year actual artificial cigarette smoke odc from twenty-six components that are th ones that mostly trigger TAARs and OR the trace amine and odorant receptors i the brain . . . His is a more neurologica scientific approach, so that it actually act on the brain more than the nose. Sound pretty fascinating.

No idea if it's doable on a larger scal

e claims it to be non-harmful when it's in ontrolled amounts and in larger space, but sked and waiting for his response.

livia Mole: The question is whether there ould potentially be any possibility of a ructural addition to the book, e.g., a page or vo that fold out into bigger spreads. So that ome chaos, interruption, etc. can literally e buried, hidden in the cleanness of the urrent book design (looking also at those yper-clean shots of the empty galleries ke the fecundity of life that exists under rock, under the floorboards, in the walls nder the surface of the ocean, etc.

I don't know exactly the imagery though ave some ideas, but if something like ldouts are definitely a no-no, I'll redirect

5 There were several ways that things could have gone, and they have gone this way.

6 They feel there is some line, that there is a doorway with many doors that can be just opened and eventually, at the end, there is a room, filled with light. There is no doorway, no room, the briskness of the weather. What am I playing at? Don't ask. Well, what is a door? They have behinds, tails, lips, butts, earlobes, neck napes, eyelids, kneecaps, elbows, skin, resplendent, and buttholes, little openings, you can unthread them this way, too, I've found, or hit them against rocks. They arrange them in the hands. They rove in all directions. They made still-fresh imprints, I finger the water round the stones. There is a rhythm, or was one, or should have been one, I cannot say. Really. Save for the red on this, near the largest swayers, it smells fantastic, my pitch, my front.

7 I remember there was a bell, for breakfast, and the food was mostly from containers and frozen, and I liked that then. I remember the nurse and her son, whom I hung out with and ate Taco Bell hot sauce with and who took me to his mother when I started seeing spots and eventually went blind probably from dehydration but it could have been from something else. I'll never forget that exact moment, walking, looking at my sneakers on the dirt, which is a deeper red than anywhere on the mainland, and then a fog, but of darkness, not blackness, came over my eyes, and I yelled, I cannot see. And I couldn't for a little while there, long enough to miss breakfast and to come to, drinking juice and eating a bagel under a blanket at the nurse's, which was under a eucalyptus tree, which shouldn't have been there but had been for a long time, the bagel was not toasted (having not gone through the toast conveyor belt, my piece, my piece) and that was that, the bagel was sweet with molasses and sugar, and I could see fine for the rest of the day but the dots in my vision stuck around, points off in the distance like arrows, nobody else could really see them. And then one day they were gone.

the thinking of the physical placing of thes
ideas.

shit or shynda?

Morag Keil: these are untested but im goir
to test some tonight so can send pics too
u want pics.

1/3 orange juice to 2/3
milk with crushed up
crackers and a spoon of
vinegar

canned vegetable soup with
half a can full of milk added
and garlic puree

oatmeal cooked and cooled
(or oat flakes) add chewed up
/ ripped tomato and cooked
chopped spinach

avocado, water, crackers,
vinegar, cooked pasta
(mashed up)

indon Johnson: In our conversations, one ey thing that Suzanne Kite and I realized that part of the struggle we were having ith what exactly to bring into the space ad to do with the fact that anything that e put into the space that wasn't a gift kind f ended this process that was fueling the ork generally. So, Suzanne asked me, "If

8 The orange fish and the dull weather. They put their hands there only to tidy themselves, when they have been at fault over the position of the construction. It is at night that great movements take place along the whole length. Sometimes above is bright red, we don't open our mouths because we don't have them. Succeed and the jowls bulge, the juleps budge, they seize the flowers in handfuls and throw them down alongside themselves. My loss is red, low in the sky, enormous. If she would just guffaw at me. They say both one and the other have this in common, that they will use whatever to wash, shiver, it barely stirs even when it is leaving. You can see them. I see them sometimes, dropping at any given moment, engaged. Who is that coming? They arrange themselves in the others' path, they evaporate without the collision. Imagine, pouncing. Who is that coming? Stumble along, hopping and uttering little cries, look, they say. I saw another today, dropping peas from one of those jellyfish. What happens in the realms of men? The fingers of their hands giving voice to a song from which no phrase emerges. Skillful at thwarting plots. Who is that coming?

9 Some Individuals.

you were to give me a gift what would be?" and this brought us to our form gifting. ~~What we'll show in the space is wall-based leather work from me that I a giving to Suzanne and~~ Suzanne will crea a wall-based rock sculpture to give to me

We have questions about how to bler our gifts into the space, the triangulatic between L. Frank, Suzanne, and I. We ar also trying to figure out how we should wor in the video footage from the flying into th installation. projection? ~~a screen?~~

Suzanne explained to me that her bas need is a sample of the chimes themselve from there she can mix something for th sound work at the museum. As for the usin of the chimes to play the song at fifteer minute intervals on Catalina, of course this i our goal, but if the logistics of it are not cos

fective with the budget we are willing to
ompromise if L. Frank receives her boulder
~~LMU~~ and her other needs are met . . .

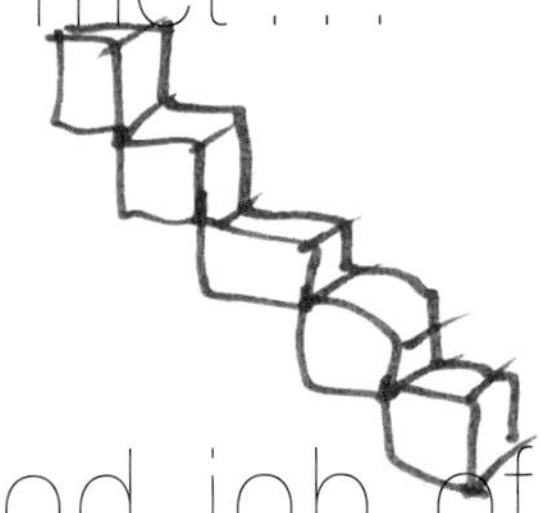

licah Silver: I didn't do a good job of
xpressing yesterday what interested me
oout the Adania Shibli text, rich in air
oetics but more than that it's a devastating
ortrait of emotional-social geometries of
olonialism, diaspora, cycles of trauma,
anscendence, misunderstanding. She's
sing language in such a specific way that
's hard to know what or how to speak
relation to it without feeling like one is
bscuring or painting over.

What comes to mind in reading it a
ew times is that for a variety of reasons, it
night lend itself well to a kind of meditative,

10 Turning, managed, preventing attachment and anything subsequent. Reversibility. They say the sea is jealous as though the sea was a singular being. Repose is what I'd scream at them. You can't avoid the land or the sea. If you cared to scream at them, and if you even had a mouth, why do you care what happens in the realms of men? Beyond meadows, oaks, turbulent. They will go barren, they're saying. I think they were stamping, we once exceeded 520 individuals. We were present to all of us, until they divided us, at random, with horses, dead eyed and under. It is still winter. Tides grow stronger always on the darkest of the cycle. Talk if you want of Obediences: Cleaning in the dark. That horse was American.

11 Was I saying it or were you? Ride them hard and put them up wet. Be aggressive, pursue the connection. Big large intakes of breath, shallow and then heavy, full, squishing, wheezing, rearing upward. How is that for a necklace? Turning. Look at us, on the seaside, we look like a glass of water, kick it over, drink me up. I'd do it again. We would! The middle is a corner between two things. I wish I could give you some evidence for the sounds they make. Don't get me goose skin, would they say it like that? I'd like to know what they're doing. Remain upright. Finish Embellishing. I'd like to stay put, but you won't let me.

spoken/scored treatment as an aud poem. Or it could be two aural gazes in the text composed on the same timelir that can never be heard simultaneous Even something like that feels a bit lik an imposition. Also, interesting to think terms of both the translation shared ar her original.

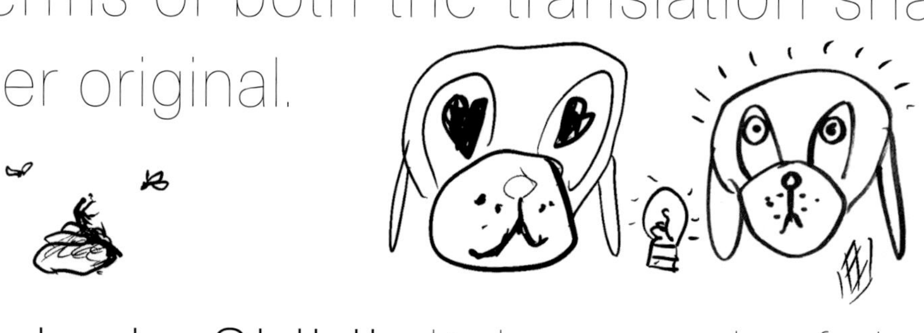

Adania Shibli: It is wonderful to kno that Micah Silver has found links with th text. How he describes it is what the tex hoped for. I'm more than happy if he doe something with it for the exhibition, awa from the literary and the linguist, to lead to places which it does not articulate, bu is being felt there, and without relying o words. This is what I understand as th rection he's planning to explore.

I certainly do not want to read the text, ot even a comma.

licah Silver: Yesterday I was listening to is wonderful Pauline Oliveros noise piece tled "No Mo," from 1966. Interesting to xperience her work with a less immediately easurable surface.

ram Moshayedi: I had wondered how or if ere might be a productive and meaningful ay of imagining Oliveros's inclusion in this ontext. Some of the thinking behind the xhibition is indebted to her ideas around e activated landscape of sound and stening.

12 There could have been other ways, but this is the way that it went. Be quiet. You're performing. That was a device. Superfluous. I can't believe the stench doesn't bother you now. Have confidence, our center is our moment of meeting, this is my chilly theater, fog and iridescent snakes at their heads and tails, solitary, folding inward, exposed, intertidal. Be careful not to seem like a monster. In lieu of a shell, I suggest tasting bad. We're stretching this. A dense mass of being in aggregate. By now there are snowbirds, seals sometimes, they have fronts.

13 What'd you say was under the earth?

14 It seems impossible even now to think about the ocean on both sides of me, as though I could be swelled upwards, and I was in some way. The next morning the boy who awoke with someone in his face.

15 Orientations.

16 It's the wind that makes the sound of the ice, and it is the wind that obscures the ice's sound.

17 See, think nothing of it.

18 From first my own memory, to Pimu as—

Andros Zins-Browne: I'm especial interested in the white ghillie suits and would be great to work with someone loc on possibilities of dying/transforming. Als depending on the color of the carpet yc use, walls, and even color of works we mig perform in front of, would be cool to crea a chameleon-like situation. I think I'll als be involved in the performances in som capacity, so we'd want to buy/fit/transforr three of these.

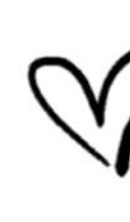

Fahim Amir: I have read the other texts quit carefully and several times; I will see if ther is a possibility to allow some connections t their thinking and poetics into the speech monologue.

~~I met Katharina Muckstein and sh~~

ready to do it in this special case, even ough she will be shooting two full movies is year. She knows about the deadline and e financial constraints. She said that she inks the main cost will be location rent nd editing. As soon as we can give her a o, she can start planning.

ina Beier: Those cats in the installation n Riga were stray cats that lived in the uilding. I have cats in the big installation n Denmark too and those are brought in aily by a cat lady. This has proved difficult s the cats need to familiarize themselves vith the space to not feel stressed and then he has to bring them in and back every ay. So to be honest it hasn't been simple. would say the best option would be to let

19 Here, something. A door whose weight you can imagine pushing, yes, open, yes, closed, yes, slamming, pulling forward. Who is in the room to greet you? Dried, yellow, the bowing and whispering of dirt on a skirt, a hemline, an ear that is becoming an arm or a clavicle, a collarbone or a little sketch of a person running towards the bed, screaming or rather streaking through the cold, a horse head, yes, it turns out it is just a sheet, and over there, that's a sponge print, I mean, it could have been. Maybe it is an opening, a big burst, a blue line. It will take you eight minutes to notice that hinge and eight minutes to notice there's a room behind the door, that the door is open a little bit or the hinge is put on poorly, that thing in the back of your throat, the horse head is a sleeve, I suppose, and I too am a big purple mass?

20 Finally. If I could sit still, I don't think I'd want to, that one layer or the taking down of many layers. That's a confusion of tongues. Don't we all quiver when it is nighttime, scratching the ground with our arms, where else would you dry your dripping clothes, moving around, not eatable, like so small, like something might have happened to them? Fishermen tell a story of two people like boxcars, they weighed them, rising, fuller, laying across each other unaware they are mixing. They might know. They do not. Do they even know you make this sound? Do you know it? Undulating. Disgusting. Don't eat that. They do seem to have certain features, and whereas they appear. And what about the last news of them? Put your implement down, there's clearly a line, wiggle, bent, altered, that must mean there is something on one side and the other side. Yes. There's one on a boat here, he's screaming. I can see his underside. You mentioned. I mean, you get it. PARADISE, PARADISE. Is what he's saying now. Out of the richness of love for the object we become the other. Enough. We'd never do that. Like how else and why. What do you see now? Some are standing still and some are lying down.

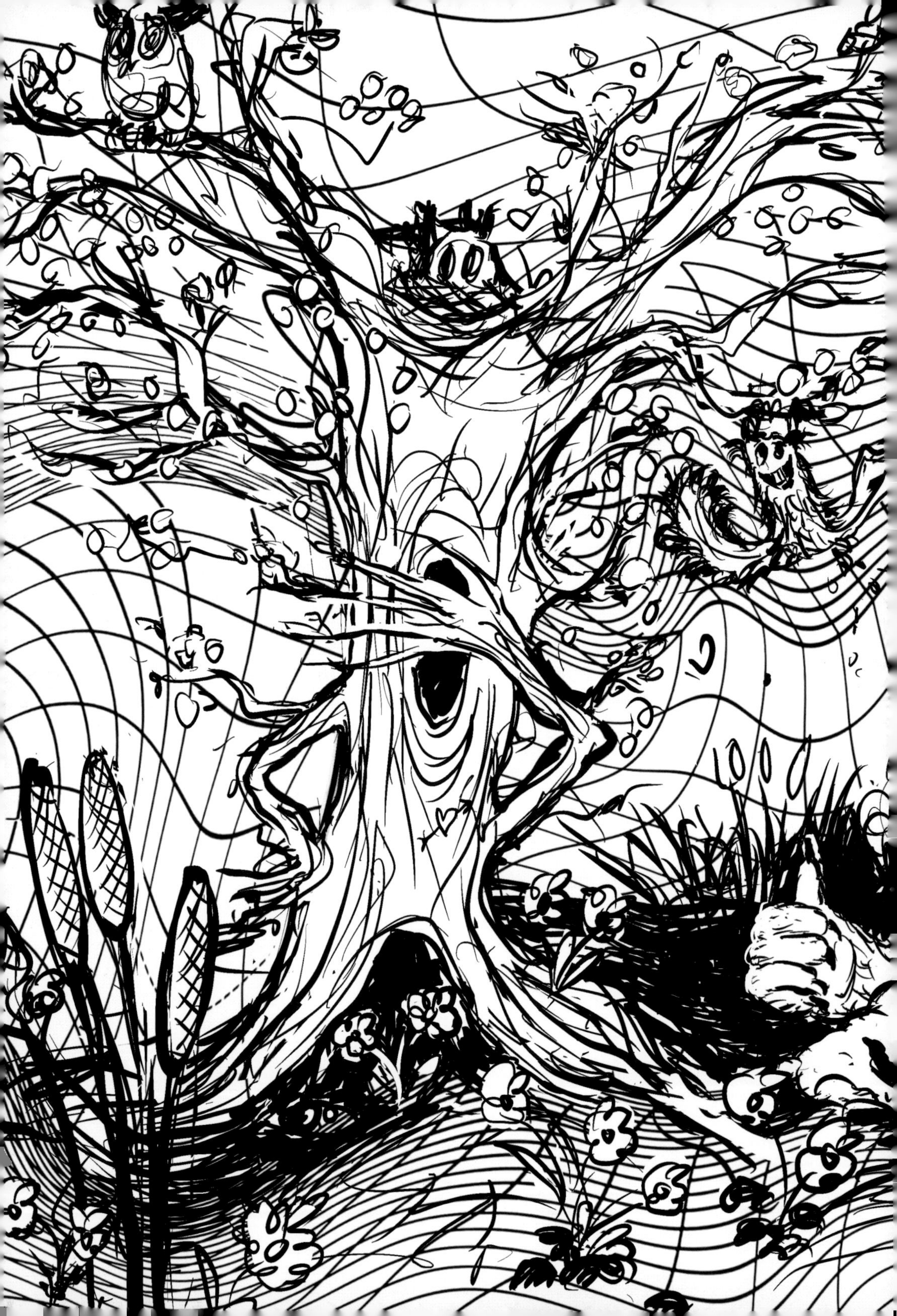

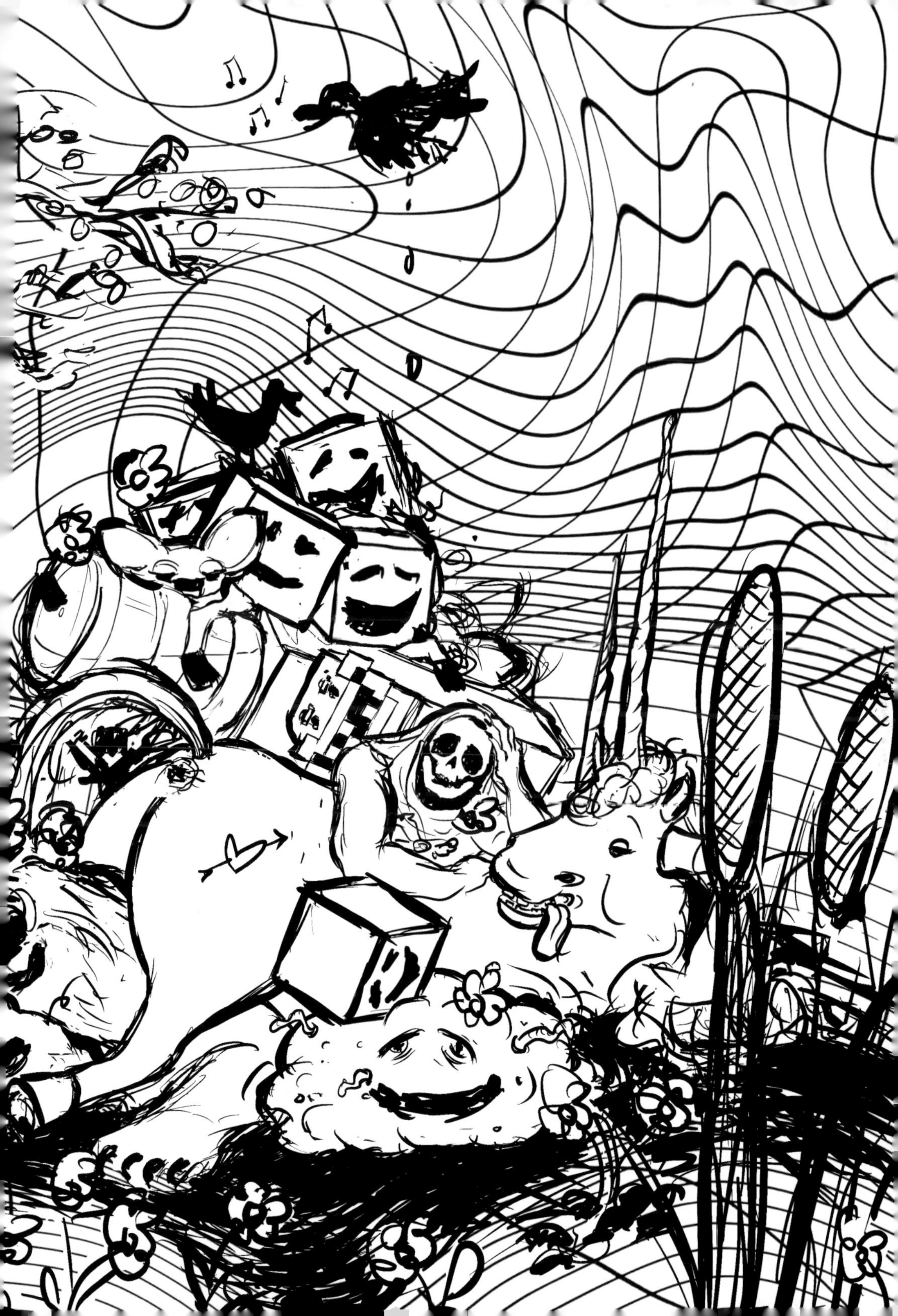

An Aesthetic Misunderstanding
or
the wind that did not see the grass that did not hear its whistle

ADANIA SHIBLI

~~cats from a shelter live in the exhibition s they don't have to travel, but then agair know there are alarms etc., so that create a whole different level of complication The cats are guaranteed trouble unless yc find a way to link it to a charity of som sort—providing a home and food for stra cats, or maybe get cat flaps installed s they can come and go! All solutions creat new problems.~~

L. Frank: so the song is called "cháamch páachum 'amáayum" and the lyrics mea "we three children are suffering, we war to run away, we want to get away." writte in mission times by children, the song wa passed along until elder ndns passed th song to a white person. he in turn carrie

until he was able to "give" it back to us.
e song has now travelled and many more
outhern calif ndns sing it. i used to sing
and feel sorrow, now i sing it and feel
rength, the strength of continuation in the
ce of holocaust.

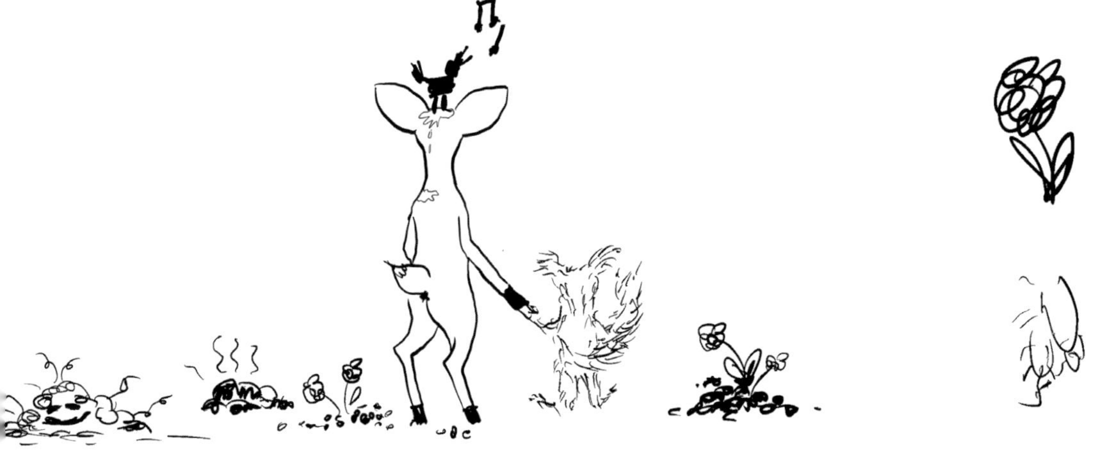

The wind blows over a tuft of grass, ruffling it, releasing a soft rustle. Entwined as they are, rustle and grass remain alien to one another. The grass cannot hear itself rustle when the wind ripples through it, and the rustle cannot see the grass from which it rose in the chafing of its blades by the wind.

Deaf as it is, the grass delights in the dance of its tall thin blades, shaking off the stillness that spells only the absence of life. Blind as it is, the wind delights in the riot of its rhythm, which sends a rumble through the air, casting off the silence that signals only the absence of life. The rustle that the grass cannot hear when the wind ruffles its blades and leaves is beautiful, and the undulation of the blades and leaves of grass as the wind ruffles them, which the rustle cannot see, is beautiful.

Blind beauty, deaf beauty.

And it is in the nature of wind to be in constant motion, born of the convergence and mixing of opposites, hot and cold, so it is in the nature of blind wind to embrace without fear the tuft of deaf grass as it brushes past. And it is in the nature of grass to be in constant endurance, born of the wind transporting pollen from another tuft, and so it is in the nature of deaf grass to stand without fear in the path of blind wind as it persists.

And the wind goes on blowing over the grass, the blades at every moment varying their rustle as they dry, as the wind carries off whatever moisture clings to these blades, their pores straining all the while to secrete fresh quantities of moisture into their atmosphere to keep them from drying out. The grass will strain and strain until it starts to droop and wilt, becoming dry and brittle as the wind keeps up its motion.

And the grass goes on persisting before the wind, its breeze at every moment varying in force as it slows down, as the grass chafes against it and resists, the wind straining all the while to swerve away to keep itself in motion. The wind will strain and strain until its force starts to wane and its direction is reversed, its whistle becoming slow and feeble as the grass persists.

Until the wind uproots the grass and carries it over the earth and casts it into the depths of the sea, stilling its motion. Until the grass escapes the wind and leaves the earth and shelters in the sea, stilling its rustle. But the sea is heaving, and from the depths the grass looks at the agitated surface and thinks the wind has followed it. The wind did not follow the grass into the sea. The wind is merely always on the move, preceded by its whistle, making it known that it will never be able to see the grass, regardless of its hiding in the depths of the sea. Except that the grass does not hide in the depths of the sea but rather lands slowly on its floor, which it takes to be dry land. And the grass cannot, in the sea any more than outside it, hear the wind whistling, just as it could not hear before the rustle of its own leaves.

But the grass sees the heaving surface of the sea, which strikes fear in the pores of its leaves, sending a shiver up its stems, draining its color. The constant movement of the grass in the depths of the sea inflames the heaving motion of its surface. And the sea heaves and heaves, pushing the wind in every direction, inflaming in its turn the anger of the wind that pushed around the surface of the sea. It is a law of nature that what you have done will be done unto you, an eye for an eye and a tooth for a tooth. It is a law of nature that if you counter wrong with wrong, no time will ever come to do what's right, so to whoever took your right eye, turn your left, and to whoever took your front teeth, open wide your mouth to let them take the back.

Blind beauty, deaf beauty.

The heaving sea pushes the grass up to its surface. Waves drive the tuft of grass onto dry land, totally dry. Sea salt has smothered the grass, turning it pale. The wind descends on it, envelops it, and carries it away from the water, drying it all the while, reviving its rustle. But now the rustle has turned rough, the sound produced by the leaves of a tuft of grass turned pale and dry, which the blind wind cannot see, and therefore it cannot know the reason for the rustle's change of state. The grass clings to the wind, holds tight and merges with it, gives up resisting, and lets it slip between the leaves that start to dance again. But now the dance has turned clumsy, the motion made by a wind turned weak and faint, which the deaf dancing leaves of grass cannot hear, and therefore they cannot know the reason for their change of state.

Blind beauty, deaf beauty.

And let us remember that grass is everywhere, and the wind descends on everything, and so it is with beauty.

The blindness of the wind and the deafness of the grass become forever entwined in the ears and under the gaze of one another. Since then, the two have lived in utter misunderstanding.

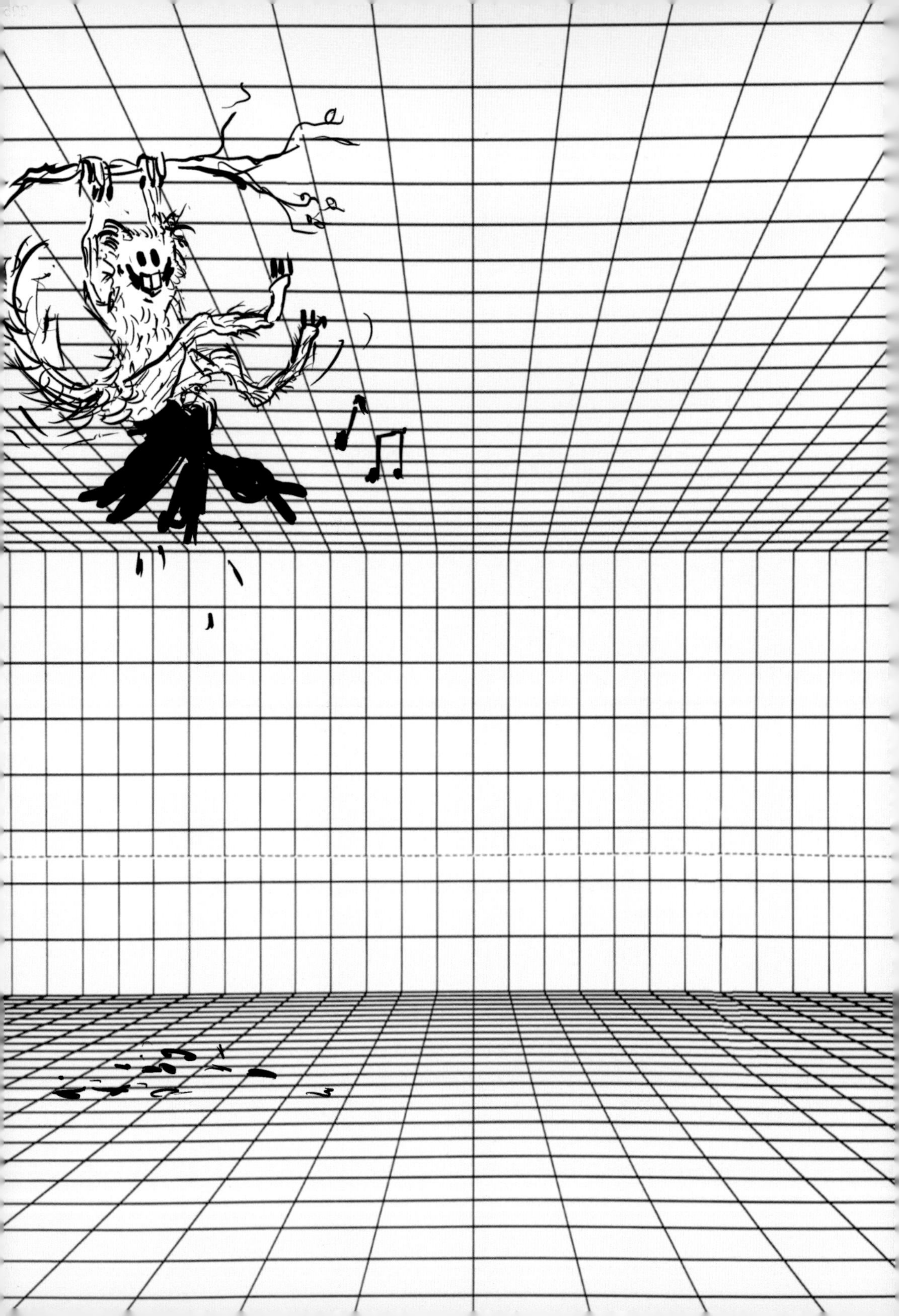

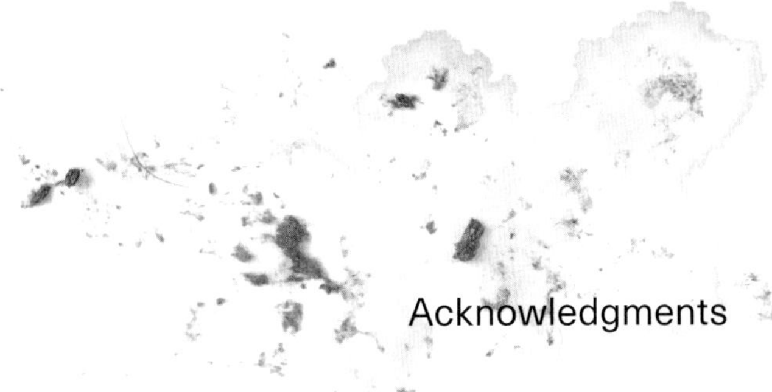

Acknowledgments

The content and scope of this project emerged from the process of its organization. An assembly of voices contributed to its making—official contributors and countless others who lent their intellect, insight, and expertise to the more-or-less invisible labor that goes into the planning of exhibitions and publications. The project benefited from the people within the museum who dedicate themselves to this line of work and others whose particular knowledge in various creative and professional fields adds layers of meaning that are as profound as they are immaterial.

I would like to start by acknowledging the contributions that form the spine of *Lifes*. The question of authorship was key to many conversations that initiated the project. Our desire was not to do away with attribution but rather to ask what role it serves in the context of exhibitions. Though some of the artists' works in the exhibition are situated within or in close proximity to the works of others, lines of individual intent are still clearly discernable. The names that make up *Lifes*—Fahim Amir, Holland Andrews, Elke Auer, Kevin Beasley, Nina Beier, Dwayne Brown, Dora Budor, L. Frank, Charles Gaines, Ley Gambucci, Piero Gilardi, Jules Gimbrone, Paul Hamilton, Asher Hartman, IONE, Shannon Jackson, Cooper Jacoby, Rindon Johnson, Darrell Jones, Morag Keil, Justin F Kennedy, Jessika Kenney, Bob Kil, Kite, Wayne Koestenbaum, Ralph Lemon, Adam Linder, Olivia Mole, Roderick Murray, Mariama Noguera-Devers, Nima Nourizadeh, Okwui Okpokwasili, Pauline Oliveros, Aubrey Plaza, Senyawa (Rully Shabara and Wukir Suryadi), Adania Shibli, Micah Silver, Samita Sinha, Greg Tate, Mike Taylor, Rosemarie Trockel, and Andros Zins-Browne—represent an assembly of individuals whose thinking informs all aspects of the exhibition and the channels of distribution it inhabits. I feel a personal indebtedness to each artist, writer, choreographer, dancer, musician, composer, philosopher, and designer included; all are integral parts of an exhibition that could have taken an infinite number of other forms. In particular, I want to recognize the role that

Adam Linder played in the planning. Early in the process, we decided that Adam would serve a dramaturgical function within the exhibition. Adam's expertise and knowledge of dance and performance history contributed in meaningful ways that pushed me to challenge my own expectations for the exhibition.

Curatorial assistant Nicholas Barlow has been a key organizational force and confidant throughout his time at the Hammer. It has been a great pleasure working together, and I am impressed by how enthusiastic and willing he has been at every turn in the planning of this project. He faced every challenge with care and attentiveness, and *Lifes* would be nothing without his invaluable presence in it.

It has been particularly heartening to witness the willingness of the museum's staff to immerse themselves in all aspects of the *Lifes* cosmology. Their commitment to the work of artists is evidenced by the quality and care that runs throughout all aspects of the presentation at the Hammer. The museum's staff is bound together as a collaborative force of its own variety, and I couldn't be happier to work alongside a team that so thoroughly prioritizes artists as the lifeline of the institution. Director Ann Philbin offered her support of this project from its nascent stage. She deferred to the process and allowed the organizational structure to emerge organically. This is a rare approach within American museums, and I am grateful that she was willing for the Hammer to take a different approach to the work we do. Colleagues within the museum's curatorial department offered their unique perspectives at various stages of the exhibition's planning; I am grateful to Vanessa Arizmendi, Nika Chilewich, Erin Christovale, and Ikechúkwú Casmir Onyewuenyi. The department is led by chief curator Connie Butler, whose deep knowledge and experience have been a benefit to me since we began working together in 2013. Connie is a leader in the field, and I am fortunate to learn from her each and every day at the Hammer. Cynthia Burlingham, deputy director of curatorial affairs, contributed valuable insights and institutional wisdom that will stay with me in the years to come. Sarah Gnirs and Miranda Cain, the curatorial department's administrative coordinators, provided much-needed logistical assistance at every step along the way. Melanie Crader, director of exhibition and publication management, must be thanked, once again, for her steadfast patience. Her enthusiasm for each contribution to this exhibition and publication provided much needed encouragement. The Hammer is fortunate to have Adam Peña, manager of exhibition design and production, and exhibition design assistant Emilio Bustos interfacing with all aspects of the exhibition's design and fabrication. Jim Fetterley, museum and theater technical director, took on a substantial role overseeing the audiovisual needs of the exhibition. We couldn't be more assured in the careful handling of artworks by chief preparator Jason Pugh, assistant preparators Michael Terzano and Angelica Perez-Aguirre, and the part-time members of the crew. Portland McCormick, director of registration and collections management, oversaw all facets of the installation, and her team, comprised of Susan Chin and Emma Rudman, were helpful for all manner of coordination. In particular, Linda Yun was the lead registrar on the exhibition, and she was accommodating beyond compare.

Without the assistance of the following individuals, *Lifes* would not have been possible: Michael Harrison, deputy director, finance, operations, and administration; Fred Yeries, deputy director, external affairs; Reshma Bishnoi, director, legal affairs; Russell Davis, chief of human resources, equity, and engagement; Veridiana Pontes, chief development officer; Courtney Raterman Casal, director, foundations and special projects; Kelly Connors, assistant manager, annual giving; Jessica Vrazilek, manager, individual giving; Sara Friedman, grant writer; Belén Pena, manager, membership; Dylan King, development associate; Alexander Barrera, manager, events; Scott Tennent, chief communications officer; Mitch Marr, associate director, communications and marketing; Nancy Lee, senior manager, public relations; Tara Morris, senior graphic designer; Lauren Graycar, graphic designer; Gabriel Noguez, senior media producer; Tim Ferris, theater production supervisor; Michael Monahan, associate director, technology; Phon Tran, audio visual supervisor; Claudia Bestor, director, public programs; and Henry Clancy, director, operations. Other museum staff from the departments of Academic Programs, Communications, Curatorial, Development, the Director's Office, Exhibition Registration and Preparation, Finance, the Hammer Store, Operations and Facilities, Public Programs, Security, Technology, and Visitor Experience commit their time and efforts to the Hammer's mission, and I couldn't be more appreciative that their many talents have been applied toward bringing *Lifes* to fruition.

The accompanying publication is intended to be an entity unto itself. It does not document or represent *Lifes* as it will exist at the Hammer. Instead, the publication is something of a record of the time that preceded the exhibition. The abbreviated account of *Lifes*, for instance, reflects the conversations that transpired until the book went to press. The list of contributors on the cover and in the biographies conveys the names involved up to a certain point, but there will surely be unforeseeable additions that respond to the needs of the exhibition as it continues to evolve. The commissioned texts by Fahim Amir, Asher Hartman, Rindon Johnson, and Adania Shibli are the basis from which this endeavor began. They were commissioned with the idea of the catalogue in mind and in anticipation that their words would serve as the basis of the exhibition. Scholarly contextual essays by Shannon Jackson and Greg Tate provide a framework through which we might be able to understand the broader issues and concerns at the heart of this exploration. I appreciate their willingness to write for the publication with little more than our conversations to guide them. Tiffany Malakooti's design brought the authors' texts to life in new ways; her candidness and openness to working through the process has informed the way I have come to think about the exhibition and the ideas that initiated it. Olivia Mole's illustrations for the catalogue, which frame one's view onto the larger whole, are part of a pervasive engagement with the avenues of publicity and mediation that surround the exhibition. I owe a debt of gratitude to Mary DelMonico, Karen Farquhar, and the team at DelMonico Books • D.A.P. for their ongoing support of the Hammer's series of publications, of which this is proudly a part. I am also appreciative of everyone at die Keure who oversaw the printing. Elizabeth Pulsinelli began working with me as an editor in 2012. She has become essential to how I think about the writing process, and I cannot express adequately how much I am indebted to her for challenging me to become a clearer and more concise writer. Additional proofreading by Rachel Walther aided in the editorial oversight. This publication would not be possible without the additional coordination of Lesley Phlek, who filled in for Claire Dilworth, former project manager of exhibitions and publications, upon her departure from the Hammer.

We appreciate the lenders who kindly agreed to part with their works for the duration of the exhibition: Hauser & Wirth; Rindon Johnson; Galerie Michel Rein, Paris/Brussels; and Sprüth Magers.

Many others were instrumental to the process of organizing the project. I appreciate the many introductions that were made on behalf of myself and Nicholas as we sought out potential collaborators. Equally important were those who offered expertise or helped to facilitate the production of works for the exhibition. I list a few of those people here: Lawrence Abu Hamdan, Kelly Akashi, Christophe Albertijn, Elisa Wouk Almino, Brando Báez Rodríguez, Justin Beal, Christine Meleo Bernstein and Armyan Bernstein, Sarah Blakley-Cartwright, Jenny Borland, Elaine Carberry, Taja Cheek, Hana Cohn, Fiona Connor, Jules Cooch, Guido Costa, Maisey Cox, Emily Craycraft, Rachel Day, Carla Donauer, Brendan Dugan, Mimi Dwyer, Chris Dyson, Alden Ehrenreich, Peter Eleey, Janiva Ellis, Olivia Erlanger, James Fauntleroy, Mario García Torres, Mariah Garnett, Nyah Ginwright, Mishuana Goeman, Piero Golia, Lizzie Gorfaine, Donatien Grau, Bruce Hainley, Trulee Hall, Juliana Halpert, Mark Handforth, Maria Hassabi, Luziah Hennessy, Hannah Hoffman, Hou Hanru, Geoffrey C. Howes, Chisa Hughes, Every Ocean Hughes, Judy Hussie-Taylor, Zenas Hutcheson, Laura Hyatt, Allie Ihm, Arthur Jafa, Alice Joubert-Nikolaev, Adam Kanter, Brooke Kanter, Anna Kats, Courtney Kivowitz, Karyn Kohl and Silas Dilworth, Barbara Kruger, Rahel Lebsekal, Isabel Lewis, Ben Lucas, Maurice Marciano, Olivia Marciano, Richard Massey, Leslie and Bill McMorrow, Matt Mehlan, Marla and Jeffrey Michaels, Casper Mills, Sohrab Mohebbi, Audrey Moyer, Shahryar Nashat, Susan Bay Nimoy and Leonard Nimoy, Silke Otto-Knapp, Anne

Palopoli, Christodoulos Panayiotou, Bettina Pérez, Amy Poncher, Zachary Poncher, Puppies Puppies (Jade Kuriki Olivo), Michael Queenland, Sean Raspet, Michel Rein, Will Richards, Darren Romanelli, Devin Ronneberg, Miljohn Ruperto, Eliza Ryan, Mark Sandelson and Nirvana Bravo, Chara Schreyer and Gordon Freund, Yasmine Seale, Gary Stuart Settles, Joni Sighvatsson, Ann Soh Woods, Celine Song, Jiwon and Steven Song, Darren Star, Joseph Stewart, Amanda Stoffel, Meg Stuart, Ali Subotnick, Josefine Thom, Hamza Walker, Ben Weyerhaeuser, Chloe Wyma, Bedros Yeretzian, and Gary Yost.

Organizations, businesses, scholars, and university affiliates that contributed to *Lifes* include Florence Bagneris, Frank Voelkl, and Justin Welch of Firmenich; Roger Bensinger of Prolitec, Inc.; Mike Ellis, Laura Machado, Teagan Machado, and Paul Romo of Connolly-Pacific Co.; AJ Valdez of Avalon Freight Services; Nanelle Gauthier, Andrew Meyers, Leonardo Rodriguez, and Michael Sweet of Air Tube Transfer Systems, Inc.; Callum Gray and Richard Prevost of LaVision Inc.; Juan Corral, Basil Katz, Henry Murphy, Sakinah Scott, Patricia Vasquez, and Andrea Whittier of Cinnabar; Gail Fornasiere and Johnny Sampson of the Catalina Island Museum; Charlie Canby and Jani Eisenhut of the Catalina Chimes Tower Foundation; Victoria Sork of the UCLA Mildred E. Mathis Botanical Garden; Desireé Reneé Martinez of the Pimu Catalina Island Archaeology Project; Joe Arvai, John Francis Heidelberg, and Kathryn Royster of the Wrigley Institute for Environmental Studies, University of Southern California; Nandita Garud, Colin T. Kremer, and Pamela Yeh of the Department of Ecology and Evolutionary Biology, University of California, Los Angeles; Jack Gilbert of the Department of Pediatrics & Scripps Institution of Oceanography, University of California, San Diego; Tim McClintock of the Department of Physiology, University of Kentucky; and Ladan Shams of the Multisensory Processing Lab, University of California, Los Angeles.

The combined efforts of those listed here represent an intellectual and creative network that imparted itself onto this project.

–Aram Moshayedi, Robert Soros Senior Curator

BIOGRAPHIES

Fahim Amir (b. 1978, Tehran, Iran) is a philosopher and author. His parents are from Afghanistan, and he lives in Vienna. Amir has taught at universities and art academies in Europe and Latin America; his research explores the thresholds of nature, culture, and urbanism; art and utopia; and colonial historicity and modernism. Amir was scientific curator of Live Art Festival, Kampnagel, Hamburg (2013); organizer of *Salon Klimbim: Feeding vegetarian tigers-entertaining utopian sensibilities*, Secession, Vienna (2014); and the Symposia for New Music, Darmstädter Ferienkurse, Darmstadt, Germany (2016). Amir co-edited *Transcultural Modernisms* (Sternberg Press, 2013), provided the afterword to the German translation of Donna Haraway's *The Companion Species Manifesto* (Merve, 2016), and recently wrote the play *Virus im Pelz*, performed at Burgtheater, Vienna (2020). Amir founded and ran the bar Schnapsloch and the publishing house Proll Positions. His book *Schwein und Zeit: Tiere, Politik, Revolte* (Edition Nautilus, 2018) received the Austrian Karl Marx Award, was included in the top ten nonfiction bestseller list of *Die Zeit/ZDF*, and was chosen as one of the best books of the year by the Goethe-Institut and the Frankfurt Book Fair. It has been translated into English as *Being and Swine: The End of Nature (As We Knew It)* (Between the Lines, 2020), into Farsi as شورش جانوران (Elm, 2021), and is forthcoming in French translation (Editions Divergences, 2022).

Holland Andrews (b. 1988, Orange, CA) is a New York-based vocalist, composer, and performance artist whose work focuses on the abstraction of operatic and extended-technique voice. Frequently highlighting themes of vulnerability and healing, Andrews arranges music for voice, clarinet, and electronics. Andrews also develops and performs soundscapes for dance, theater, and film, and their work has toured internationally with artists such as Bill T. Jones, Dorothée Munyaneza, Will Rawls, and Demian Dinéyazhi. Notable musical collaborations include Son Lux, Christina Vantzou, William Brittelle, Peter Broderick, and Methods Body. Andrews's most recent EP, *Wordless* (2021) was released on the label Leiter, spearheaded by Nils Frahm and Felix Grimm.

Elke Auer (b. 1980, Vienna) is a Vienna-based artist and theatrical stage designer. She works with text, still and moving image, and bodies and their representation. She exhibits regularly in international contexts and has curated several group exhibitions for the feminist art association Vereinigung bildender Künstlerinnen Österreichs in Vienna. Since 2015, she has been developing MODERN HOLES, a long-term, research-based project that is attempting to map the anxiety states of her generation along the lines of urbanism, alienation, vulnerability, shame, pop culture, hip-hop, sticky ideals, bio-politics, and constructions of masculinity and femininity.

Nicholas Barlow (b. 1989, Los Angeles) is a curatorial assistant at the Hammer Museum, where he has recently assisted on the exhibitions *Paul McCarthy: Head Space, Drawings 1963–2019* (2020) and *Tishan Hsu: Liquid Circuit* (2020), as well as projects by artists David Hartt and Ho Tzu Nyen. Previously, he was a curatorial assistant at the Los Angeles County Museum of Art, where he helped organize projects including *3D: Double Vision* (2018), *Alejandro G. Iñárritu: CARNE y ARENA* (2017), *Guillermo Del Toro: At Home with Monsters* (2016), and *Robert Mapplethorpe: The Perfect Medium* (2016).

Kevin Beasley (b. 1985, Lynchburg, VA) lives and works in New York. Beasley's practice spans sculpture, photography, sound, and performance. Recent exhibitions, installations, and performances include Prospect.5, New Orleans (2021); Performa 2021 Biennial, New York; *The Dirty South: Contemporary Art, Material Culture, and the Sonic Impulse*, Virginia Museum of Fine Arts, Richmond (2021); *Grief and Grievance: Art and Mourning in America*, New Museum, New York (2021) and A4 Arts Foundation, Cape Town, South Africa (2020); *ASSEMBLY*, the Kitchen, New York (2019); the Studio Museum in Harlem, New York (2016); the Renaissance Society at the University of Chicago (2016); the Solomon R. Guggenheim Museum, New York (2015); and the Museum of Modern Art, New York (2012). Recent solo exhibitions include *A View of a Landscape*, Whitney Museum of American Art, New

York (2018–19); *Kevin Beasley*, Institute of Contemporary Art, Boston (2018); and *Hammer Projects: Kevin Beasley*, Hammer Museum, Los Angeles (2017). He received his BFA from the College for Creative Studies, Detroit, in 2007, and his MFA from Yale University School of Art, New Haven, CT, in 2012.

Nina Beier (b. 1975, Aarhus, Denmark) is a Danish artist living and working in Copenhagen and Berlin. Solo exhibitions of her work have been presented internationally, at Rønnebæksholm, Denmark (2021); Kunsthal Gent, Belgium (2019); Spike Island, Bristol, United Kingdom (2018); Kunstverein Hamburg (2015); Contemporary Art Centre, Vilnius, Lithuania (2015); Yerba Buena Center for the Arts, San Francisco (2010); and other venues. Her work has been included in group exhibitions at institutions such as High Museum of Art, Atlanta (2019); YUZ Museum, Shanghai (2018); Kunsthaus Zürich (2018, 2009); Walker Art Center, Minneapolis (2016); Institute of Contemporary Arts, London (2016, 2009); KW Institute for Contemporary Art, Berlin (2015); Centre Pompidou, Paris (2014, 2013); Tate Modern, London (2012, 2007); and Hamburger Bahnhof, Museum for Contemporary Art, Berlin (2011).

Dwayne Brown (b. 1985, Bronx, NY) is a dancer and performer currently based in Harlem, New York. In addition to numerous appearances in film, television, and various stage productions, he has worked as a professional modern dancer with Bill T. Jones/Arnie Zane Dance Co., Ralph Lemon, Sean Curran, Reggie Wilson/F&H Performance Group, and most recently Kevin Beasley. Brown is represented by Clear Talent Group.

Dora Budor (b. 1984, Zagreb, Croatia) is a New York-based artist and writer. Her recent and forthcoming solo exhibitions include Kunsthaus Bregenz, Austria (2022); Galleria d'Arte Moderna e Contemporanea, Bergamo, Italy (2022); Progetto, Lecce, Italy (2021); Kunsthalle Basel, Switzerland (2019); 80WSE, New York (2018); and Swiss Institute, New York (2015). Her work has been presented in numerous group exhibitions, including at the Migros Museum, Zurich (2021); Schinkel Pavillon, Berlin (2021); Kunstmuseum Winterthur, Switzerland (2021); MoMA, Warsaw, Poland (2020); MO.CO Panacée, Montpellier, France (2020, 2018); Kunstverein Nuernberg, Germany (2019); Kunsthaus Centre d'art Pasquart, Biel, Switzerland (2018); Louisiana Museum of Modern Art, Humlebaek, Denmark (2017); Palais de Tokyo, Paris (2017); K11 Art Museum, Shanghai (2017); MOCA Belgrade, Serbia (2017); Whitney Museum of American Art, New York (2016); Swiss Institute, New York (2016); Museum Fridericianum, Kassel, Germany (2015); and Halle für Kunst und Medien, Graz, Austria (2015). She participated in the 58th October Salon, Belgrade Biennale, Serbia (2021); Tbilisi Biennial, Georgia (2021); 2nd Riga International Biennial of Contemporary Art, Latvia (2020); Geneva Sculpture Biennale (2020); 16th Istanbul Biennial (2019); 13th Baltic Triennial, Lithuania (2018); Vienna Biennale (2017); and 9th Berlin Biennial (2016). Budor was a recipient of the Rema Hort Mann Foundation's Emerging Artist Prize in 2014 and Pollock-Krasner Foundation Grant in 2018. In 2019, she was awarded a Guggenheim Fellowship in Fine Arts.

L. Frank (b. 1952, Santa Monica, CA) is a Tongva-Ajachmem artist, writer, tribal scholar, cartoonist, and community activist who lives and works in Santa Rosa, CA. Her work has been exhibited widely throughout the United States and Europe. She is the author of *Acorn Soup* (Heyday Books, 1999), a collection of her illustrated column of the same name that appeared regularly in the quarterly newsletter *News from Native California*. She has served on the board of directors for the California Indian Basketweavers Association, Advocates for Indigenous California Language Survival, and the Cultural Conservancy. Frank was awarded the Alexis Arquette Family Foundation LA Pride 2 Spirits Activist Award (2019) and the Traditional Bearers for Biocultural Diversity Fellowship by the Seventh Generation Fund for Indigenous Peoples (2018). She was an artist-in-residence at the Headlands Center for the Arts, Sausalito, CA (1990). She studied with Sister Corita Kent at Immaculate Heart College in Los Angeles.

Los Angeles-based artist **Charles Gaines** (b. 1944, Charleston, SC) produces works in a range of media that investigate how rules-based procedures construct order and meaning. He has been the subject of several solo exhibitions, most recently at San Francisco Museum of Modern Art and Dia: Beacon (both 2021). *Charles Gaines: Gridwork 1974–1989*, a survey of Gaines's early works, was organized by the Studio Museum in Harlem and traveled to the Hammer Museum, Los Angeles (2015). In 2012, Gaines was the subject of a mid-career survey at the Pomona College Museum of Art and the Pitzer College Art Galleries, Claremont, CA. In 2013, he received a John Simon Guggenheim Memorial Foundation Fellowship, and he received the 60th Edward MacDowell Medal in 2019. He currently lives and works in Los Angeles and, since 1989, has been an influential educator at the School of Art at the California Institute of the Arts, where he recently launched a scholarship to promote diversity in the MFA art program.

Ley Gambucci (b. 1995, San Diego) is a caretaker and fugitive in flight and transition.

Piero Gilardi (b. 1942, Turin, Italy) is an artist, writer, and activist who lives and works in Turin. A foundational figure of the Arte Povera movement, Gilardi has presented sculptures, paintings, and installations at international galleries and museums since the mid-1960s, including in the landmark exhibitions *When Attitudes Become Form* (Bern, Switzerland, 1969) and *Op Losse Schroeven* (Amsterdam, 1969), where he also served as an advisor to the exhibition curators. Since the late 1960s, Gilardi's essays and art criticism have been published in *Flash Art* and other publications. He has published two books: *Dall'arte alla vita, Dalla vita all'arte* (*From Art to Life, from Life to Art*) (La Salamandra, 1981) and *Not for Sale* (Mazzotta, 2000). In 2008, Gilardi opened the Parco Arte Vivente (Park of Living Art), an open-air sculpture park and interactive museum in Turin. In 2017, Gilardi was the subject of a retrospective at MAXXI-National Museum of 21st Century Art in Rome, entitled *Nature Forever.*

Jules Gimbrone (b. 1982, Pittsburgh) is a New York-based composer and visual artist who creates sculptures and installations that synthesize physical and sonic material and investigate sensory perception. Gimbrone's work has appeared internationally in a variety of venues, including the Walker Art Center, Minneapolis (2018); SculptureCenter, New York (2018); the Roy and Edna Disney/CalArts Theater (REDCAT), Los Angeles (2018); and LAXART, Los Angeles (2014).

Paul Hamilton (b. 1967, Kingston, Jamaica) is a Bessie-nominated dancer who trained at the Jamaica School of Dance and SUNY Purchase. In 2000, he began collaborating with Reggie Wilson / Fist and Heel Performance Group, creating five original works from 2003 to 2014. With choreographer Keely Garfield, he created four works from 2005 to 2016. In 2014, he began a collaboration with Ralph Lemon that led to *Scaffold Room*; he received a Bessie nomination for this and for performances with Garfield and Jane Comfort. In 2018 and 2019, he performed in two Bessie-winning productions by Comfort and David Thomson, as well as *Bruce Nauman: Disappearing Acts* and *Judson Dance Theater: The Work Is Never Done* at the Museum of Modern Art, New York. An excerpt of his solo *The Sitch* was performed at Danspace Project Gala (2019).

Asher Hartman (b. 1959, San Francisco) is a transgender writer, director, and maker of live performances who currently lives in Los Angeles. His works, which combine strategies of theater and performance art, grapple with social and political issues in an era of chronic crisis. His dense, visual, poetic, and embodied texts—infused with clown and cringe humor and evidence of trance and psychic journeying—are set in engulfing installations designed to disorient, unnerve, and elicit strong feeling. Hartman is the director and founder of Gawdafful National Theater, a loose association of visual artists, actors, and performance artists. Recent Gawdafful performances include the long-form project "The Dope Elf," a series of traveling performances and films that was supported in large part by The Lab, San Francisco, and Yale Union, Portland, OR. A great deal of Hartman's theatrical work was developed with the support of Machine Project, Los Angeles, from 2010 to 2017. X Artists' Books published his first collection of plays, *Mad Clot on a Holy Bone*, in 2020.

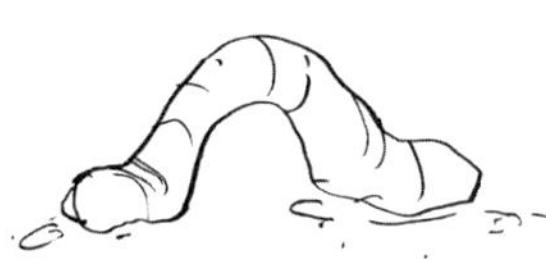

IONE (b. 1937, Washington, DC) is an author, director, and improvisational text and sound artist. For over three decades, she taught and performed internationally with her creative partner and spouse Pauline Oliveros. IONE has authored nonfictional books, including *Pride of Family: Four Generations of American Women of Color, Nile Night: Remembered Texts from the Deep, Listening in Dreams*, and *This is a Dream!* She also has edited two volumes of personal essays entitled *Spell Breaking: Anthologies of Women's Mysteries.* She has written and directed several plays and operas that feature music and sound design by Oliveros, including *Njinga the Queen King, Io and Her and the Trouble with Him*, and *The Lunar Opera: Deep Listening For_Tunes*, and directed the film *Dreams of the Jungfrau.* In 2013, IONE and Oliveros presented a scene from *The Nubian Word for Flowers, A Phantom Opera* at the Hammer Museum in Los Angeles. In April 2020, IONE presented Oliveros's *World Wide Tuning Meditation*, a virtual event created with MacArthur Fellow Claire Chase and Raquel Klein of Music on the Rebound and the International Contemporary Ensemble.

Shannon Jackson (b. 1967, Manhattan Beach, CA) is Hadidi Professor at the University of California, Berkeley, where she holds appointments in the departments of Rhetoric, History of Art, Art Practice, and Theater, Dance, and Performance Studies. She is a scholar of contemporary art, performance, media art, and social practice, and her books and collaborative projects include *Social Works* (Routledge, 2011), *Public Servants* (MIT Press, 2016), *The Builders Association* (MIT Press, 2015), In Terms of Performance, Valuing Labor in the Arts (with *Art Practical*), and a special issue of *Representations* devoted to time-based art. Jackson has received many awards, including a 2015 Guggenheim Fellowship. She serves on the boards of several museums and arts organizations and is a founding board member and program director for the Kramlich Art Foundation.

Cooper Jacoby (b. 1989, Princeton, NJ) is an artist based in Miami and Los Angeles. Recent solo exhibitions include Fitzpatrick Gallery at The Intermission, Piraeus, Greece (2022); Central Fine, Miami (2019); High Art, Paris (2018); Freedman Fitzpatrick, Los Angeles (2017); Swiss Institute at LUMA Westbau, Zurich (2017); Staatliche Kunsthalle Baden-Baden, Germany (2016); and a two-person exhibition with Rosa Aiello at KW Institute for Contemporary Art, Berlin (2016). His work has been included in group exhibitions at Le Plateau, Frac Île-de-France, Paris (2019); Fondation Villa Datris, L'Isle-sur-la-Sorgue, France (2019); and the Swiss Institute, New York (2019).

Rindon Johnson (b. 1990, San Francisco) is an artist and poet whose work is based on language. He has presented solo exhibitions at Chisenhale Gallery, London; Julia Stoschek Collection, Düsseldorf, Germany; and the SculptureCenter, New York. Johnson has participated in group exhibitions at the Brooklyn Museum, New York; Kunstverein Freiburg, Germany; The Studio Museum in Harlem, New York; Literaturhaus Berlin; Haus der elektronischen Künste, Basel, Switzerland; and other venues. He is the author of *Nobody Sleeps Better Than White People* (Inpatient, 2016); the VR book *Meet in the Corner* (Publishing House, 2017); *Shade the King* (Capricious, 2017); and *The Law of Large Numbers: Black Sonic Abyss* (Chisenhale, Inpatient, and SculptureCenter, 2021). He was born on the unceded territories of the Ohlone people. He lives in Berlin.

Darrell Jones (b. 1969, Washington, DC) has performed with a variety of choreographers and dance companies, including Urban Bush Women, Ronald K. Brown, and Min Tanaka, and he has long-term collaborative relationships with Bebe Miller Company and Ralph Lemon. He is a tenured faculty member at the Dance Center of Columbia College, Chicago, where he teaches classes in physical practice, performance, and improvisational techniques.

Morag Keil (b. 1985, Edinburgh, Scotland) is an artist based in London. She has had solo exhibitions at the Institute of Contemporary Arts, London (2019); New Bretagne Belle Aire, Essen, Germany (2016); Cubitt Gallery, London (2013); and Palais de Tokyo, Paris (2011). Her work has been included in exhibitions at Yale Union, Portland, OR; Kunsthaus Glarus, Switzerland; Stadtgalerie, Bern, Switzerland; Fondazione Prada, Venice, Italy; Swiss Institute, New York; and others.

Justin F. Kennedy (b. 1983, Boston) is a Berlin-based dance and vocal artist, teacher, and DJ, raised in St. Croix, US Virgin Islands. Kennedy's research evolves from experiences and analyses of trance dance and its further translatability into workshops, science fiction operas, durational dance installations, and film. Notable projects include *Vorglühen, OUT NOW*, Uferhallen, Berlin (2021); *UNFURL the jukebox musical: a shareable cypher*, Montag Modus, Radialsystem, Berlin (2021); *UNFURL: a lucid science fiction*, 11th Berlin Biennale, Martin Gropius Bau, Berlin (2020); and *Some Murder Theatre in Here*, Volksbühne Grüner Salon, Berlin (2020). They have performed intimately with and for Emma Howes, Ligia Lewis, Louis Vuitton, Tino Sehgal, Adam Linder, Liz Kinoshita, Jeremy Shaw, Josh Johnson, BODYSNATCH, Faustin Linyekula, Jeremy Wade, Peaches, Wu Tsang, and others.

Jessika Kenney (b. 1976, Spokane, WA) is unwinding and nourishing a harbor of voices through performance, recording, writing, and conversation. Her recent work includes *Anchor Zero*, a voice- and video-based installation, presented at the Frye Art Museum in Seattle (2015), and *ATRIA* (2015), an LP inspired by the poetry of Attar of Neyshabur and the mantras attributed to Sunan Kalijaga, released by SIGE Records. Her acclaimed collaboration with Eyvind Kang includes works for orchestra and voice, including performances by the BBC Scottish Symphony Orchestra and the Greek Radio Symphony Orchestra, as well as many records, including *Reverse Tree* (Black Truffle, 2016), *The face of the earth* (Ideologic Organ, 2012), and *Aestuarium* (Ideologic Organ, 2005). She was awarded the inaugural James W. Ray Distinguished Artist Award in 2014 and the Lionel Hampton Vocal Jazz Award in 1992.

Bob Kil (b. 1975, Seoul) has spent the past twenty-five years in London and Berlin. Kil works within the realm of language, employing written and spoken words, and introduces vocal and physical rhythms into performances. Often working with other professionals, including artists, dancers, and techno DJs, they appropriate the format of poetry reading and borrow the vocabulary of pop culture. Kil has delivered performance pieces at various institutions, such as Thorvaldsens Museum, Copenhagen (2021); Holstebro Museum, Denmark (2021); Aeromoto, Mexico City (2020); KW Institute of Contemporary Art, Berlin (2019); Kunsthal Gent, Belgium (2019); DRAF x O2 Forum, London (2018); Le Plateau, Frac Île-de-France, Paris (2018); South London Gallery (2016); and Art Sonje, Seoul (2014). Kil runs bobshop, a space for performances and readings in Berlin.

Kite (aka Suzanne Kite) (b. 1990, Sylmar, CA) is an Oglála Lakȟóta artist and composer raised in Southern California. Kite's scholarship and practice highlight contemporary Lakota epistemologies through research-creation, computational media, and performance. She has a BFA from CalArts in music composition, an MFA from Bard College, and is a PhD candidate at Concordia University, where she is a research assistant for the Initiative for Indigenous Futures. She is a 2019 Pierre Elliott Trudeau Foundation Scholar, a 2020 Tulsa Artist Fellow, and a 2020 Women at Sundance x Adobe Fellow. Kite lives and works in Montreal and Tulsa.

Wayne Koestenbaum (b. 1958, San Jose, CA)—poet, critic, novelist, artist, performer—has published twenty-two books, including *The Cheerful Scapegoat, Figure It Out, Camp Marmalade, My 1980s & Other Essays, The Anatomy of Harpo Marx, Humiliation, Hotel Theory, Circus, Andy Warhol, Jackie Under My Skin*, and *The Queen's Throat* (nominated for a National Book Critics Circle Award). His most recent book is *Ultramarine*, the third volume of his trance trilogy, published by Nightboat Books. In 2020, he received an American Academy of Arts and Letters Award in Literature. Yale's Beinecke Rare Book and Manuscript Library acquired his literary archive in 2019. His first piano and vocal record, *Lounge Act*, was released by Ugly Duckling Presse Records in 2017. He is a distinguished professor of English, French, and Comparative Literature at the City University of New York Graduate Center.

Ralph Lemon (b. 1952, Cincinnati, OH) is an artist, writer, and choreographer.

Adam Linder (b. 1983, Sydney) is a choreographer working in Los Angeles and Berlin. In exhibition format or on stage, his work engages with facets of performing arts: dance, text, and costume. His recent solo exhibitions have taken place at the Museum of Modern Art, New York (2020); South London Gallery (2018); and Kunsthalle Basel, Switzerland (2017). In 2018, the CCA Wattis Institute for Contemporary Arts in San Francisco organized the survey exhibition *FULL SERVICE*, which traveled to Mudam, the Contemporary Art Museum of Luxembourg (2019). Linder's stage works have been presented at HAU Hebbel am Ufer in Berlin; Kampnagel, Hamburg; Roy and Edna Disney/CalArts Theater (REDCAT), Los Angeles; Sadler's Wells, London; and others. Linder received the Mohn Award for artistic excellence as part of *Made in L.A. 2016: a, the, though, only*, at the Hammer Museum, Los Angeles.

Olivia Mole (b. 1975, London) is a Los Angeles-based artist who works in drawing, video, sculpture, animation, VR, and performance. She has presented solo and collaborative exhibitions and performances at such venues as Riviera Parking, Santa Barbara, CA (with Ian Byers-Gamber) (2021); JOAN, Los Angeles (2017); Cloaca Projects, San Francisco (2017); and the CCA Wattis Institute for Contemporary Arts, San Francisco (2015). She also has participated in group exhibitions at Montclair State University Galleries, Montclair, NJ (2021); Tiger Strikes Asteroid, Los Angeles (2020); Los Angeles Contemporary Archive (2019); LAXART, Los Angeles (2019); Human Resources, Los Angeles (2018); and Gas Gallery, Los Angeles (2018); among others. Mole worked from 1998 to 2009 in art direction and set design for live action and animation production studios, including DreamWorks Animation, Warner Brothers, and the BBC.

Aram Moshayedi (b. 1981, Barstow, CA) is a writer and the Robert Soros Senior Curator at the Hammer Museum in Los Angeles.

Roderick Murray (b. 1965, New York) is an award-winning designer, creator, and supporter of live performance, working since 1982. Collaborators include Ralph Lemon, Kimberly Bartosik/daela, and Beth Morrison Projects, where he is the director of production.

Mariama Noguera-Devers (b. 1994, Los Angeles) has been dancing and performing since the age of five in styles of Trinidad and Tobago folk and the Graham technique. She has also studied ballet, West African, hip-hop, and dancehall. She holds a bachelor of arts in dance from the New School and has taught Soca Fitness to all ages at after-school programs and dance studios throughout New York City.

Nima Nourizadeh (b. 1977, London) is an acclaimed film, commercial, and music video director. He is a graduate of Central St. Martins in London. In 2005, Nourizadeh directed a breakthrough clip for Hot Chip's single "Over and Over," followed by award-winning videos for such artists as Lily Allen, Chromeo, Flight of the Conchords, and Santigold. In 2008, he won Best Director at the UK Music Video Awards, and in 2010 he teamed up with producers Todd Phillips and Joel Silver to direct his first feature film, *Project X*. In 2015, Lionsgate released Nourizadeh's second film, *American Ultra*, starring Jesse Eisenberg and Kristen Stewart. More recently, Nourizadeh has directed for television, including episodes for *Little America* and *Gangs of London*.

Okwui Okpokwasili (b. 1972, New York) is a New York-based writer, performer, and choreographer who is constantly collaborating with a constellation of artists invested in somatic transmissions and deep entanglements in live performance.

The life and work of composer, performer, and humanitarian **Pauline Oliveros** (b. 1932, Houston, d. 2016, Kingston, NY) was committed to opening her own and others' sensibilities to the many facets of sound. Beginning in the 1960s, she influenced American music through her work with improvisation, meditation, electronics, myth, and ritual. Many credit her as the founder of present-day meditative music. All of Oliveros's work emphasizes musicianship, attention strategies, and improvisational skills. Deep Listening, her lifetime practice, was fundamental to her composing, performing, and teaching. A recipient of the John Cage Award and the William Schuman Award, she received many honors in her lifetime, including four honorary doctorates. She served as Distinguished Research Professor of Music at Rensselaer Polytechnic Institute in Troy, NY, and Darius Milhaud Artist-in-Residence at Mills College, Oakland, CA, among other appointments. She was the founder of Deep Listening, now housed at the Center for Deep Listening at Rensselaer.

Aubrey Plaza (b. 1984, Wilmington, DE) is an actress, comedian, writer, and producer. On television, she starred in the critically acclaimed television series *Parks and Recreation* (2009–15) and FX and Marvel's *Legion* (2017–19). She has also starred in and produced several films, including *Ingrid Goes West* (2017), for which she won Best First Feature at the Independent Spirit Awards, *Black Bear* (2020), and *The Little Hours* (2017). Other film credits include *Dirty Grandpa* (2016), *Mike and Dave Need Wedding Dates* (2016), *Safety Not Guaranteed* (2012), *Scott Pilgrim vs. the World* (2010), and *Funny People* (2009). She cocreated Evil Hag Productions and recently cowrote the children's book *The Legend of the Christmas Witch* (Viking Books, 2021).

Senyawa (founded 2010, Yogyakarta, Indonesia) is an experimental band from Indonesia comprised of Rully Shabara and Wukir Suryadi. Incorporating homemade instruments and deft vocal explorations, the duo creates compositions that embody elements of traditional Indonesian music, free jazz, noise, and heavy metal. Senyawa has performed at venues and festivals worldwide, including MONA FOMA Festival in Tasmania (2015). In 2018, a selection of their original compositions appeared on the soundtrack of the blockbuster videogame *Red Dead Redemption 2*. In 2021, in an act of "decentralized" distribution, Senyawa released the album *Alkisah* through over forty international record labels simultaneously.

Adania Shibli (b. 1974, Shibli, Palestine) has written novels, plays, short stories, and narrative essays. She has been awarded the A M Qattan Foundation Young Writer of the Year Award twice: in 2001, for her novel *Masaas* (Al-Adab, 2002; translated as *Touch*, Clockroot, 2009), and in 2003, for her novel *Kulluna Ba'id bethat al Miqdar aan el-Hub* (Al-Adab, 2002; translated as *We Are All Equally Far from Love*, Clockroot, 2012). Her latest novel, *Tafsil Thanawi* (Al-Adab, 2017, translated as *Minor Detail*, Fitzcarraldo Editions, London, and New Directions, New York, 2020), was shortlisted for the National Book Award and nominated for the International Booker Prize. Shibli is also engaged in academic research and has been teaching part time since 2012 at Birzeit University, Palestine. In the fall of 2021, she was Friedrich Dürrenmatt Guest Professor for World Literature at the University of Bern, Switzerland.

Micah Silver (b. 1980, Sylva, NC) is an artist, writer, and producer based in Los Angeles. Silver has episodically presented installations, audio works, and diagrams in contemporary art and educational contexts since 2002. His book *Figures in Air: Essays Toward a Philosophy of Audio* (2014) is now in its second printing with Inventory Press. Other writings on art and social concern have been published by *Art Los Angeles Reader*, *ArtEast Magazine*, the Okayama Art Summit, Politics on Medium, and Museo Universitario Arte Contemporáneo, Mexico City (CDMX). As an advocate for creators and platforms that elevate experimental takes on listening, music, and acoustics, Silver worked with Diapason Gallery, New York, from 2003 to 2006. From 2006 to 2012, he was a founding curator at Experimental Media and Performing Arts Center, Rensselaer Polytechnic Institute in Troy, NY; in 2020, he opened Black Hole, a listening room and audio nonprofit in south Los Angeles.

Artist and composer **Samita Sinha** (b. 1978, Queens, NY) investigates voice, the body, and consciousness through the raw material of vibration.

Greg Tate (b. 1957, Dayton) is a writer, musician, and cultural provocateur who lives on Harlem's Sugar Hill. His books include *Flyboy in the Buttermilk* (1992); *Midnight Lightning: Jimi Hendrix and the Black Experience* (2003); *Everything But the Burden: What White People Are Taking from Black Culture* (2004); and

Flyboy 2: The Greg Tate Reader (2016). His appearances as a commentator in documentary films about James Brown and Miles Davis and in Ahmir Thompson's *Summer of Soul* have been widely acclaimed. Tate is a proud member of Howard University's Bison Nation and has been visiting faculty at Yale University, Columbia University, Brown University, Williams College, Princeton University—where he taught "The Loud Black and Proud Musicology of Amiri Baraka"—and New York University, where he debuted the course "A Brief History of Woke Black Music." In 2022, Duke University Press will publish *White Cube Fever: Writings and Conjurations on the Dark Arts*, a collection of Tate's writings on visual culture.

Mike Taylor (b. 1960, Dallas, TX) writes, directs, and produces video, audio, theater, and art installations. Her live work has been presented at the Kitchen, the Ontological, PS122, Dixon Place, La MaMa, TONIC, and various raw spaces throughout New York. Her videos have been shown in the United States and Europe, most recently at the Whitney Museum of American Art, New York, as part of a series by and about DanceNoise.

Since the early 1980s, **Rosemarie Trockel** (b. 1952, Schwerte, Germany) has worked across media to challenge the concept of male artistic genius and investigate contemporary and historical discourses concerning artistic and social identity. Her first exhibitions took place in 1983 at the galleries Monika Sprüth, Cologne, and Philomene Magers, Bonn, Germany. Recent solo exhibitions include *The Same Different*, Moderna Museet Malmö, Sweden (2018–19); *Reflections/Riflessioni*, Pinacoteca Giovanni e Marella Agnelli, Turin, Italy (2016–17); and *Märzôschnee ûnd Wiebôrweh sând am Môargô niana më*, Kunsthaus Bregenz, Austria (2015). The survey exhibition *A Cosmos* was presented at Museo Nacional Centro de Arte Reina Sofia, Madrid (2012); New Museum, New York (2012–13); and Serpentine Gallery, London (2013). In 2005, the Museum Ludwig, Cologne, and MAXXI, Rome, presented Trockel's retrospective exhibition *Post-Menopause*. In 1999, she became the first woman to represent Germany at the Venice Biennale, and, in 1997, she participated in documenta X in Kassel, Germany. She was awarded the Goslarer Kaiserring award in 2011 and the Roswitha Haftmann Prize in 2014. She currently lives and works in Berlin and Potsdam, Germany.

Andros Zins-Browne (b. 1981, New York) is an artist working at the intersection of performance and dance. Central to these pursuits is the exploration of the body as material and immaterial, a site of exchange between embodied images and somatic experience. His recent choreographic work extends into interactions with singers, considering the voice as a body. Zins-Browne has presented solo performances at Institute of Contemporary Arts, London (2019); Fondation Galeries Lafayette, Paris (2018); Whitney Museum of American Art, New York (2017); Rockbund Art Museum, Shanghai (2017); and other institutions. Additionally, he has presented several remixes of existing works, including those by Jérôme Bel, Simone Forti, and Tony Cokes. He is the recipient of grants and awards from the Goethe Institute, the Flemish Cultural Ministry, New York State Council on the Arts, and the Graham Foundation for Advanced Studies in the Fine Arts. He lives and works in New York.

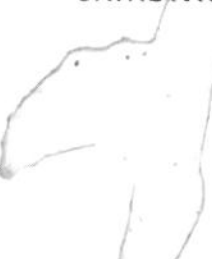

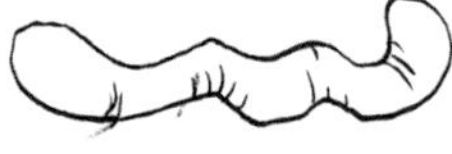

This book was published on the occasion of the exhibition *Lifes*, organized and presented by the Hammer Museum, Los Angeles, February 13–May 8, 2022.

The exhibition was organized by Aram Moshayedi, Robert Soros Senior Curator, with Nicholas Barlow, curatorial assistant.

Major support for *Lifes* is provided by Chara Schreyer and Gordon Freund with generous funding from Christine Meleo Bernstein and Armyan Bernstein, the Danielson Foundation, Karyn Kohl and Silas Dilworth, Leslie and Bill McMorrow, Susan Bay Nimoy and Leonard Nimoy, Mark Sandelson and Nirvana Bravo, Jiwon and Steven Song, and Darren Star. Additional support is provided by the Danish Arts Foundation, the Knox Foundation, Maurice Marciano Family Foundation, Marla and Jeffrey Michaels, Ben Weyerhaeuser, Ann Soh Woods, and an anonymous donor.

Published in 2021 by the Armand Hammer Museum of Art and Cultural Center, Inc., and DelMonico Books • D.A.P.

Hammer Museum
10899 Wilshire Boulevard
Los Angeles, CA 90024-4201
310-443-7000
www.hammer.ucla.edu

Distributed worldwide by
DelMonico Books • D.A.P.

ARTBOOK | D.A.P.
75 Broad Street, Suite 630
New York, NY 10004
artbook.com
delmonicobooks.com

Director, Exhibition and Publication Management: Melanie Crader
Project Managers: Claire Dilworth and Lesley Phlek
Designer: Tiffany Malakooti
Editor: Elizabeth Pulsinelli
Proofreader: Rachel Walther
Typefaces: Eidetic Modern and Neue Haas Unica Pro
Papers: GardaPat Kiara, Favini Bindakote, Senses, and Igepa IBO One
Printer: die Keure Printing, Bruges, Belgium

Illustrations by Olivia Mole, 2021.

Adania Shibli's "An Aesthetic Misunderstanding or the wind that did not see the grass that did not hear its whistle" was translated from the Arabic by Yasmine Seale. Fahim Amir's "Stealing Colors" was translated from the German by Geoffrey C. Howes.

The quote by Charles Gaines from *No Title: The Collection of Sol LeWitt* appeared in Michael Ned Holte's essay "Differential Equations: The Art of Charles Gaines," in *Artforum* (October 2011).

Library of Congress Control Number: 2021921572

ISBN: 978-1-63681-047-8